CW00588988

BOSSMEN:

BILL MONROE & MUDDY WATERS

BY JAMES ROONEY

A DA CAPO PAPERBACK

Library of Congress Cataloging in Publication Data

Rooney, Jim, 1938-
  Bossmen: Bill Monroe & Muddy Waters.

  (A Da Capo Paperback)
  Originally published: New York: Dial Press, 1971.
  1. Monroe, Bill, 1911–   . 2. Muddy Waters, 1915–   . 3. Musicians—United
States—Biography. 4. Music, Popular (Songs, etc.)—United States—History and
criticism. I. Title. II. Series.
ML394.R66   1991   784.5'3'00922 [B]   85-3736
  ISBN 0-306-80427-1

This Da Capo Press paperback edition of *Bossmen: Bill Monroe & Muddy Waters* is
an unabridged republication of the edition published in New York in 1971, with
author emendations. It is here reprinted by arrangement with Doubleday.

Published by Da Capo Press, Inc.
A Subsidiary of Plenum Publishing Corporation
233 Spring Street, New York, N.Y. 10013

*This book is dedicated
to my Uncle Jim Flaherty,
architect, painter, free spirit,
and friend to young people.*

ACKNOWLEDGMENTS

In the words of a recent poet, "I get by
with a little help from my friends."
This book is the product of my friendship
with Bill Monroe and Muddy Waters. Each
man has been forthright and cooperative and
hospitable. I interviewed Bill on the road in
Canada, New Jersey, and Virginia, and at
home in Nashville in the early months of
1970. His remarks about Clea Baze and
Arnold Schultz first appeared in the program book of the 1969 Newport Folk
Festival Program Book and were recorded
by Alice Foster and Hazel Dickens who
have my thanks. Needless to say, Earl
Scruggs, Don Reno, Bill Keith, Kenny
Baker, and Ralph Rinzler were also most
helpful. Many early pictures of Bill were
provided by Ralph and by Mrs. Tex Logan.
I interviewed Muddy Waters in the hospital
in Champaign-Urbana, Illinois, shortly
before Christmas of 1969 and subsequently
at his house in Chicago in the early months
of 1970. Willie Dixon, Buddy Guy, Bob
Messinger, and Paul Butterfield were also
very generous with their time.
Finally, thanks to Bob Cornfield for his
interest and support, Carol Futterman for
her ability to transfer my illegible scrawl
to the typewritten page, and my wife Sheila
for putting up with the mess in the living
room.

INTRODUCTION

Every field has its "bossman"—the one who sets the style, makes the rules, and defines the field in his own terms. In the world of bluegrass and early country music the man is Bill Monroe. In the world of urban blues and blues bands — Chicago blues — the man is Muddy Waters.

Bill and Muddy have remarkably similar careers. Both came from rural areas where they grew up listening to the natural music around them. For Monroe it was square dance music, church music, the blues guitar of a colored man named Arnold Schultz, and, above all, the fiddle playing of his Uncle Pen Vanderver. For Muddy it was string-band music, the sound of the harmonica, church music, preaching, but, above all, the sound of the blues as played and sung by such men as Robert Johnson and Son House—the raw sound of Mississippi Delta blues. Both men brought their music to the city and the structured world of commercial music—Bill to Nashville and Muddy to Chicago. There each man began to work with what he brought with him to give it a new shape, a new style, that would speak to a new time and new situations. Each man formed a band, and each man's band became a school to the best musicians in the style. These musicians went on, in turn, to form their own bands, and, in time, the worlds of bluegrass and blues bands took shape.

The contemporary musical scene is eclectic if nothing else. Today's young musicians absorb musical influences from all over the world. Very often, they themselves have little or no personal musical background. Everything they play is borrowed from somewhere. This is especially true of whites whose personal musical heritage might have ended with a grandfather who sang or a cousin that played. That old European folk music was washed out of them as they grew up in America. Even young blacks, though into "soul" heavily, are cutting off from their musical roots in the church and the blues singers. It becomes increasingly rare to find someone who has been isolated enough from other

9

musical forms to be able to develop and maintain a style that is totally self-contained. Both Bill Monroe and Muddy Waters are such men. Each has a deep awareness of the value of the culture he sprang from and has done his best to be true to it while at the same time expanding upon it and developing it to a point where it could flourish and survive in the commercial musical world. Each man has a deep professional commitment to his music which is reflected in the way he plays and works with the men around him. Each man has come a long way from where he started, driven by the knowledge that it was his mission in life to make the best music he could out of the materials he inherited. Each man has discovered that his music seemed to get deeper and more meaningful with the passing of the years, and this awareness has given him a renewed determination to pursue his music further.

In this book you will be listening to each man tell his story. Listen carefully, for in their voices you will find keys to the men. They talk the way they are. Each man is aware of who he is and exactly what he has done. Each man has thought deeply about his music and respects his music. Music has been for each a way of getting at what is true and real in life. For each, music is life.

CONTENTS

DISCOGRAPHY/BILL MONROE

The best way to read this book is with some musical interludes. Both Bill Monroe and Muddy Waters have had long, rich, musical careers, and the book is intended to be a companion piece to their music. Unfortunately, record companies don't always keep the records in their catalogues that you would like, and some confusion arises when old records appear with new covers, groupings, and titles, but I will try to list what is currently available.

Bill Monroe: Bluegrass 1950-1958–*BCD 15423*
Issued as a 4-CD set by the German-based Bear Family Records. Contains 109 selections digitally remastered as well as an excellent 65-page booklet co-authored by Charles K. Wolfe and Neil Rosenberg. An invaluable collection. A follow-up is planned covering Bill's recordings into the sixties.

Columbia Historic Edition—*COL FC 38904*
Contains many early classics, including "Kentucky Waltz," "Blue Yodel #4," "Bluegrass Special," Lester Flatt and Bill on "Toy Heart," "I'm Going Back To Old Kentucky," and "Mother's Only Sleeping." Excellent notes by Bob Allen.

Bill Monroe/Flatt & Scruggs—*Rounder RND 06*
Includes most of the "classic" band with Flatt, Scruggs, and Chubby Wise, notably, "Heavy Traffic Ahead," "Little Cabin Home On The Hill," "Bluegrass Breakdown," "Will You Be Lovin' Another Man."

Classic Bluegrass Recording, Vol. I—*County CCS 104*
Another excellent collection of early "classics," including "Travelling This Lonesome Road" with Mac Wiseman and Bill, "Goodbye Old Pal," "Along About Daybreak," "The Old Crossroad." Informative notes by Douglas Green and quotes from Bill about the songs and his music.

The High Lonesome Sound—*MCA 110*
Includes much material from the early fifties with Jimmy Martin and Rudy Lyle: "On and On," "Memories of Mother and Dad," "When The Golden Leaves Begin To Fall." Also Carter Stanley and Bill on "Sugar Coated Love," and Ed Mayfield on "My Little Georgia Rose with three fiddles: Gordon Terry, Red Taylor, and Charlie Cline. This album is also distinguished by complete notes by Ralph Rinzler.

All Time Greatest Hits—*Columbia PC-1065*
Lives up to its title: "Blue Moon Of Kentucky," "Rose of Old Kentucky," "Girl in the Blue Velvet Band," "Footprints in the Snow," "I Hear a Sweet Voice Calling," and many more.

I Saw The Light—*MCA 527*
Includes many fine hymns from the fifties period, especially "I'll Meet You In The Morning," "I've Found A Hiding Place," "Lord, Build Me A Cabin In Glory."

Bluegrass Time—*MCA 116*
Includes fine material from the sixties featuring Peter Rowan, Richard Greene, and Lamar Grier on "Turkey in the Straw," "Midnight On The Stormy Deep," "I Wonder Where You Are Tonight," and "Dusty Miller."

Greatest Hits—*MCA 17*
Includes "Muleskinner Blues," "Molly and Tenbrooks," "Rawhide," "Uncle Pen," "Roanoke." A fine collection of Bill's most requested songs.

Best of Bill Monroe—*MCA 4090*
Another good collection including "Pretty Fair Maid In A Garden," "First Whipoorwill," "The Little Girl and The Dreadful Snake," and many others.

Uncle Pen—*MCA 500*
One of Bill's finest albums, featuring his long-time fiddler Kenny Baker playing fiddle tunes which Bill learned from his Uncle Pen. Includes "Methodist Preacher," "Jenny Lynn," "Dead March," and "Goin' Up Caney."

to: David Gahr

Beanblossom—*MCA 2-8002*
A double album recorded "live" at Bill's park in Indiana with guests Jimmy Martin, Jim and Jesse, Earl Scruggs, and many former bluegrass boys. Captures the feel of a bluegrass festival.

Master of Bluegrass—*MCA 818*
An album which demonstrates that Bill is still creating exciting, original music in his seventies. Includes "Old Ebenezer Scrooge," "Go Hither, Go Yonder," "Lady of the Blue Ridge," and the haunting "My Last Days On Earth."

Other albums available are:

Bill Monroe and Friends—*MCA 5435*
Designed to show off Bill with many of today's "stars." Not always a musical success, but contains good duets with Ricky Skaggs, Emmy Lou Harris, and John Hartford.

Bill and Charlie Monroe—*MCA 124*
Includes "No One But My Darlin'," "Poison Love," "I'm Old Kentucky Bound."

Country Music Hall of Fame—*MCA 140*
Includes "Muleskinner Blues," "Get Up John," and "Rocky Road Blues."

Kentucky Bluegrass—*MCA 136*
Includes "I Live in the Past," "Log Cabin in the Lane," "Sally Goodin'," "Kentucky Mandolin."

Bluegrass '87—*MCA 5970*
Contains one of Bill's best songs of recent years "Bluest Man In Town," as well as some fine instrumentals such as "Long Bow" and "Old Brown County Barn."

Southern Flavor—*MCA 42133*
Takes Bill's sound into the digital age. A fine representation of Bill "live" in the studio. Produced By Emory Gordy, Jr.

Bill Monroe: Live At The Opry: Celebrating 50 Years On The Grand Ole Opry—
MCAD 42286
A live recording showing that Bill continues to play with energy and creativity.

Any attempt to list all the records featuring Bill Monroe's various sidemen would be an unrealistic project. Suffice it to say that Flatt & Scruggs have many records on Mercury and Columbia, with a good deal of their best early material re-released on Rounder. The Stanley Brothers also have a fine re-release on Rounder. The bulk of their material will be found on King/Starday, now part of Gusto Records. Don Reno and Red Smiley's records are also on King/Starday. Mac Wiseman's records are on RCA, Gusto, and CMH. Jimmy Martin's are on MCA and Gusto. The Osborne Brothers can be found on MCA, Rounder, and CMH. Kenny Baker has made several records for County. Bill Keith records for Rounder Records, as do Richard Greene and Byron Berline. Byron Berline is also on several Flying Fish albums. Peter Rowan has records on Flying Fish and Sugar Hill. Ricky Skaggs records for CBS and has excellent albums on Sugar Hill and Rounder as well.

DISCOGRAPHY / MUDDY WATERS

Many of Muddy's records were on the Chess label. Happily, MCA Records is in the process of reissuing much of the Chess material, including the following:

Muddy Waters Boxed Set—*CH 80002*
The definitive collection of Muddy's entire career at Chess. Contains extensive notes by Mary Katherine Aldin and Robert Palmer.

Chess is also re-releasing many of the original albums, including:

The Real Folk Blues—*CH 9274*
Includes "Screamin and Cryin'," "Gypsy Woman," "Little Geneva," Willie Dixon's classic "Mannish Boy," and "Same Thing."

More Real Folk Blues—*CH 9278*
More of Muddy's best from the early fifties including "Honey Bee," "Sad Letter," "Down South Blues," "Too Young To Know."

The Best of Muddy Waters—*CH 9255*
Includes "I Can't Be Satisfied" from Muddy's first session, classics with Little Walter—"Rollin' Stone," "Long Distance Call," "Louisiana Blues," and Willie Dixon's "Hoochie Coochie Man" and "I Just Want To Make Love To You."

Muddy Waters Sings Big Bill Broonzy—*CH 9197*
Includes fine cuts of Broonzy's tunes adapted to the blues band style. Shows Muddy's band with James Cotton and Otis Spann at its height. "Tell Me Baby," "Southbound Train," "I Feel So Good," "Hey, Hey."

Muddy Waters Folk Singer—*CH 9261*
Includes Muddy on unamplified guitar backed by Buddy Guy: "My Home Is In The Delta," "Feel Like Going Home," "Country Boy," and Sonny Boy Williamson's "Good Morning Little School Girl."

Rolling Stone—*CH 9101*
A collection of Muddy's classics including "She Moves Me," "I Just Want To Make Love To You," "Got My Mojo Working," and others.

At Newport—*CH 9198*
A great live record, including "Hoochie Coochie Man, "Tiger In Your Tank," Got My Mojo Working," and a beautiful improvised blues by Otis Spann, "Goodbye Newport Blues."

: David Gahr

Additional releases are also planned, including:

Muddy & The Wolf—*CH 9100*
Rare & Unissued—*CH 9180*

Other records currently in print include:

Hard Again—*Blue Sky (Epic) PZ 34449*
An excellent record produced by Johnny Winter. Includes "Mannish Boy," "Bus Driver," "I Want To Be Loved," "Jealous Hearted Man," "I Can't Be Satisfied," "Little Girl."

King Bee—*Blue Sky (Epic) PZ 37064*
Another good album produced by Johnny Winter. Includes 'I'm A King Bee," "Too Young To Know," "I Feel Like Going Home," "No Escape From The Blues."

Mud In Your Ear—*Muse 5008*
A mixed bag, including "Diggin' My Potatoes," "Sad Day Uptown," "Long Distance Call."

Muddy's sidemen went on to make many records of their own, as did the young white musicians who were influenced by him. Little Walter also recorded for Chess. Chess records has recently issued a superb Willie Dixon "Boxed Set" (CH 16500) and other Willie Dixon records can be found on Columbia, Folkways, and Alligator. Otis Spann has records on Sine Qua Non and Vanguard. Junior Wells and Buddy Guy are on Sine Qua Non, Vanguard, and Blind Pig. James Cotton has records on Sine Qua Non, Arhoolie, Takoma, and Vanguard. Paul Butterfield recorded for Elektra and Bearsville, Mike Bloomfield was on Columbia and Takoma, Elvin Bishop is available on Polydor. John Hammond, Jr. has records on Vanguard and Rounder. John Mayall is available on London and Polydor. George Thorogood records for Rounder/EMI. The Rolling Stones have records on London and Rolling Stone Records.

BOSSMEN: BILL MONROE & MUDDY WATERS

BOSSMAN BILL MONROE

Bill Monroe was the youngest in his family. His people were farmers, working hard to get a living out of the hills around Rosine, Kentucky. It's pretty country there. You pass by today on the "Bluegrass Turnpike" and the hills are deceptively inviting, green, undulating waves. Pretty to look at but hard to work. Bill's mother died in 1921 when he was a boy, barely ten years old. When Bill was in his teens his older brothers went North to look for work. Bill's father died, leaving him alone at the age of seventeen. With no family to keep him there in Rosine, Bill set out to join his brothers Charlie and Birch, who were now living outside of Chicago in Whiting, Indiana.

If you was raised on a farm you would know of hard times and you didn't get things as a kid that you do now. On Saturday I would get a nickel to buy some candy with and that's all I got all week. And one pair of shoes a year and two pairs of overalls. Have shoes to wear in the wintertime and go barefooted in the summertime. If you plowed for your father it felt good to your feet to follow that plough and stay in that furrow with the fresh ground turning over there. You didn't mind.
There wasn't no radios, nothing; you didn't hear no music—just what you played—and farm work. And you wondered what life would have been like in a town or in a city, but I was afraid to tackle it. But I reckon my people figured I would never make anything there and that they should try to get me out of there to where I could make a decent living. Course my father and mother died and a little later on Uncle Pen passed away and Uncle Birch Monroe died, so there wasn't very many of the Monroes left there—just some cousins.

But Bill's imagination and his mind were still in those hills back in Kentucky.

21

As the youngest in the family he had been a little quieter and more observant than the others. His eyes were crossed and weak, but his ears were sharp and they took in all of the sounds around him. Those sounds haven't left Bill to this day, and they formed the basis for his musical development.

I have always been proud of the people I came from in Kentucky and growing up the way that I did in the country and to learn what old-time music was really all about and to study it ever since I was a young boy and then to make it do something later on in years and to originate a music.

The first music I heard was Uncle Pen and Uncle Birch and a man by the name of Clarence Wilson, and they played numbers like "Soldier's Joy." Each town maybe had a little band, you know. I knew a little band eight or ten miles from us by the name of Foster String Band—that was back in the twenties, and I remember a band that had a fiddle, a Hawaiian guitar, mandolin—they might have had a banjo. They played breakdowns, dance music and a few waltzes and a little Hawaiian music. Maybe there would be one man who would know a solo, and there was one fellow singing "Greenback Dollar."

There's a long ridge back home called Jerusalem Ridge, and I remember we had to cross that and go on down about a mile to where we come to this real old house called the Lizer place, and this man, Clea Baze that played the fiddle, he lived there. We'd walk back there with a coal oil lantern, and we got there that night and there was a good many in the room listening to them play and they sat in the middle of the room and I thought that was awful pretty music . . . numbers like "Turkey In the Straw" and that kind of stuff. They'd play "Cacklin' Hen" and he could really play that. It was something to go knowing you was going to hear some music that night.

At these gatherings the music was largely oriented toward instrumental music for dancing. On Sundays there was a different form of music—hymn singing in the old Sacred Harp way at the community singing schools. Based on a five-note scale, this music was very open, unlike the closer sound of more modern music. In secular music this open sound would be called "lonesome,"

and to the people around Rosine, that "lonesome sound" seemed to fit right with life in the mountains.
Another sound that seemed to fit in was the sound of the blues.

I remember in Rosine this colored man would haul freight from the train station to six or seven stores bringing each man what he wanted. And he would be riding his mule on those muddy roads just whistling the blues. And you could tell by the way he whistled that he was the bluest man in the world. Many days through people's lives the blues will touch them. Might not have started out on a Monday—might have been a blue Monday—but sometime through that week they'd have felt the blues. If you can sing. If you made up words as you went along you'd make them up to suit yourself, to suit the mood you was in. You would gradually touch the blues someplace.

Every boy growing up meets men that he looks up to and admires. There were two men who impressed Bill as a boy and whose music found an important place in his music as it developed. One was a black blues player who used to live near Rosine called Arnold Schultz.

The first time I think I ever seen Arnold Schultz . . . this square dance was at Rosine, Kentucky, and Arnold and two more colored fellows come up there and played for the dance. They had a guitar, banjo, and fiddle. Arnold played the guitar but he could play the fiddle—numbers like "Sally Goodin." People loved Arnold so well all through Kentucky there; if he was playing a guitar they'd go gang up around him till he would get tired and then maybe he'd go catch a train. He lived down at a little mining town—I believe it was called McHenry—or on down further. I used to listen at him talk and he would tell about contests that he had been in and how tough they was and how they'd play these two blues numbers and tie it up. And they had to do another number and I remember him saying that he played a waltz number and he won this contest. And just things like that I have never forgot. He thought it was wonderful that he could win out like that and I admired him that much that I never forgot a lot of the things that he would say. There's things in my music,

you know, that come from Arnold Schultz—runs that I use in a lot of my music. I don't say that I make them the same way that he could make them 'cause he was powerful with it. In following a fiddle piece or a breakdown, he used a pick and he could just run from one chord to another the prettiest you've ever heard. There's no guitar picker today that could do that. I tried to keep in mind a little of it—what I could salvage to use in my music. Then he could play blues and I wanted some blues in my music too, you see.

Me and him played for a dance there one night and he played the fiddle and we started at sundown and the next morning at daylight we was still playing music—all night long. And of course, that automatically made you be dancing on Sunday, but that is really the truth—I could say that I have played for a dance all night long. I played the guitar with him. I just could second fair— probably any guitar man in the country could've beaten me but anyhow I played guitar for him. I believe it was the next day about ten o'clock there was a passing train come down through and stopped at Rosine and I believe he caught that train and went back home and that was about the last time I ever saw him. I believe if there's ever an old gentleman that passed away and is resting in peace, it was Arnold Schultz—I really believe that.

From this time on Bill felt that the blues was a natural part of him and his music. It didn't seem any different from being "lonesome." It was all there together in those hills.

The other man who had a major influence on Bill at this age was his Uncle Pen Venderver.

He fiddled all of his life. To start out with, he was a farmer for a long time. There was four in his family. His wife and two children. The boy's name was Cecil and I believe he passed away first and then the daughter and the mother. And then Uncle Pen came to live with us. He would leave out on Monday morning and go through some part of the country and he would go to visit some people—he might know them, I guess. And he would have something to trade on and he would trade. He was the kind of man, you know, who needed the boots. He needed that extra change of money. Then he would go on— maybe spend a night with somebody else up the road. But he would always

make his circle. And sometimes he would start out with nothing much and come back maybe leading a cow—he always rode a horse back or a mule—and maybe he'd sell the cow to somebody and start all over again. Might have been a bad life for a lot of people, I guess. But there's not too many people who can trade and come out winners. But he was one who didn't have to come out too much, but that was his way of making a living. Later on, he got throwed by a horse and broke his hip and he was a cripple. He was on crutches the rest of his life. His last days in Kentucky, me and him would play for square dances wherever they would want a fiddle and a guitar. You know, I rode behind him and we'd take out and go back through the country maybe three or four or five miles and play for a square dance at somebody's home, you know. They'd clear a room out and me and him would play for the dance. And we'd make three or four dollars apiece, something like that. And he'd always give me just as much as he made. If it was six dollars he'd give me three of it.
It learns a boy to have someone like that to show him. It gives him experience. And at the same time my uncle was getting some enjoyment out of it.
And he had the best bow movement with a fiddle bow that you have ever seen in your life. He could really shuffle.
A lot of Uncle Pen's fiddling is in bluegrass music. It learned me how it had to be played to be good back when I was really young. You could hear him and you could tell that he could really fiddle. But if you had never heard him, the people in the community could tell you how he could fiddle. And you had to go along with them because there was that many that would tell you how he could really fiddle. So you knew when you was young that he was a wonderful old-time fiddler. It's got its part in bluegrass music.

So, for his seventeen years Bill Monroe had absorbed and retained a lot of music. He instinctively valued the culture he grew up in and learned from it. He wasn't thinking about it especially. It was just in him. At the moment he was concerned with finding Birch and Charlie and getting a job and making some money. He left his home never to return. All he needed he brought out with him.
By the late twenties, the mid-Northern cities were becoming heavily indus-trialized. The automobile industry was the cause of much of the expansion. Oil refineries, steel mills, and automobile plants needed large numbers of unskilled

laborers and found their supply in the young men fleeing the hard-pressed rural areas of the South. They came from the Carolinas, Tennessee, Alabama, Mississippi, and Kentucky—strong young men, used to hard work. They came to the factories and refineries hoping to get money for a better life than they had left behind at home. Sometimes the supply of labor was greater than the demand, and a young boy like Bill, fresh from the country, took a while to get started.

It was hard getting work when I went up there. It was ten weeks before I got a job. Birch didn't get a job for a long time, Charlie had trouble with his foreman and after a little while lost his job. So I was the only one working. There was places like Standard Oil Refinery and Sinclair. I worked there, you know. I worked in the Barrel House for close to five years.
Many's a day I stacked a thousand barrels—two thousand barrels. We could unload a freight car in forty-five minutes. There would be two inside the car and two or three of us outside and they would spin those barrels down on you and you would have to catch them—just like playing ball. And then we would clean barrels with gasoline. Some of them weighed one hundred and fifty pounds and that was some hard work, I'll tell you. I made forty cents an hour, then forty-five cents an hour. Every two weeks Charlie or Birch would come with me to get my pay. Fifty or sixty dollars was all I could seem to make. And we would pay the rent and buy groceries and I would set aside three dollars for streetcar back and forth. And I never could put any money away it seems. They hung right on. If I rode a streetcar going to a dance why they knew that I would pay the way for them to go. Every place I went they went.
I worked every day for five years and all I got out of it was I spent forty dollars for a mandolin and I got a couple of suits of clothes.
I've often wondered if I was doing the right thing. I guess I was. It wouldn't be right not to support your people.
We lived in Whiting for a short time. And then we moved over to East Chicago, Indiana—about four or five miles from there and we lived there for the rest of the time until we left the country.

While Bill was working at Sinclair there was very little opportunity to play

much music. What music he did play was with Charlie and Birch for little
house parties and dances in the area where they would make about five dollars
apiece, but there wasn't enough money in it to make it worth doing full time.
Music was fast becoming the major broadcast item on radio, however, and
WLS in Chicago had started a program featuring old-time and country music
every Saturday night. By 1932 the WLS Barndance audience had grown to
such an extent that the station sent out a traveling show to cover this listening
territory. Charlie, Birch, and Bill sensed an opportunity to make their music
pay off better than it had.

At that time you couldn't hardly get a job playing music that paid any money.
WLS in Chicago was about the only place up there that really paid any good
money, and you got very little on smaller stations without you didn't have a
sponsor, you know; they would take you in and give you so much a week. If
you went out and played for a square dance you might make three or four or
five dollars a night. We'd get maybe twenty-five dollars for the three of us or
the four of us if somebody was playing bass fiddle or something. While I
worked there at Sinclair, WLS, they wanted a road show, and they put their
people out on it that they thought would draw good, like Arkansas Wood-
chopper and people like that. And they had a set of square dancers at the
theater and they wanted a set on the road, so Charlie and Birch and me and
another feller had us a set of square dancers, you know, and we danced for
WLS on the road. I don't know how long. And they paid twenty-two dollars-
and-a-half a week. Per man. Of course that far back you could get a room for
seventy-five cents—a good room. You could get a steak for thirty-five cents.
So it was pretty good money.
I'd take off two weeks and then I'd go back. But then I got to taking off so
much that I had to finally quit the job.
We played a lot of times seven days a week. We had a Packard we would
travel in. We played mostly through Indiana and Illinois and maybe a few
days in Wisconsin and Michigan. It give us some experience and give us a
chance to travel. That's something I never had done before then, you know,
was to travel any, you might say. And all the time we was dancing, we was
practicing on the side with music and playing whenever somebody wanted us
to play.

This was Bill's first taste of being a full-time musician, and he liked it a lot better than working in the barrelhouse at Sinclair. The money wasn't bad, and his music was improving with all of the work. Originally he had taken up the mandolin as a third choice. Charlie had the guitar and Birch the fiddle, and, being the smallest, Bill had been left with the mandolin to play.

The thing I really wanted to play was the fiddle. Of course, there wasn't a chance—Birch, he was going to play the fiddle.
I really wanted to play guitar too—the way Arnold Schultz played it with a straight pick. If I'd have fooled with the guitar I would have been a blues singer and I never would have fooled with a mandolin and me and Charlie would never have worked together. It might have been a different setup all the way around. I'd probably have been a blues singer playing the guitar.

He was growing to like the mandolin though and was beginning to explore its possibilities. His rhythm playing was getting good and solid, and he was starting to play a little lead, picking out the melodic line the way he had heard it on the fiddle.

When I started to play the mandolin I wanted to be sure that I didn't play like nobody else, and I was going to have a style of my own with the mandolin. And I worked it out until it did become a style. Years ago people played a little on the mandolin just to fill in or to be playing. But to have heard really good fiddle players back in the early days—Clayton McMichen and people like that— and to really get on a mandolin and play the old-time notes that's in a fiddle number has really helped to create an original style of music on the mandolin.

When the Barndance tour finally ended, they went to work on another local radio station in Gary, Indiana—eleven dollars for six programs a week. Shortly, however, they were to find that their touring had paid off. They got a call to come out to Iowa and work there. Birch decided that traveling wasn't the life for him and he went home. But Charlie and Bill—now known as the Monroe Brothers—decided to make a go of it. The depression had started to hit hard, and they seemed to be doing better playing music than they would have trying to find regular work.

This company out of Shenendoah, Iowa, they wanted us to come out there and go to work—I believe it was called Texas Crystal Company. And we worked there for three or four or five months and then they sent us to Omaha. While we was there at Shenendoah, they had a little barn dance they had on Saturday night. It was for Henry Fields—he had a big store there and a radio station too—a thousand watts, I guess. So that give us some more experience. And then we moved to Omaha for the same company and stayed there, I guess, maybe a year, year and a half. And moved from there to Columbia, South Carolina.

It was a full three years, and Charlie and Bill found that they had gained quite a following as a result of their radio broadcasts. They weren't alone in the field by any means. There were the Callahan Brothers, the Morris Brothers, the Delmore Brothers, and many others, each with their own sound. Charlie and Bill, however, seemed to stand out from the others by virtue of their high, clear voices. Bill's tenor was way up there, and it had that "lonesome" quality along with some blues feeling that made it immediately identifiable. They had speed too, and Bill's mandolin playing was more dynamic and melodic than anyone else's playing at the time. He was creating a style on the instrument that also distinguished the Monroe Brothers from their competitors.
Soon Victor Records (the Bluebird Label) got word that the Monroe Brothers were in the Carolinas and had a following and signed them up.

Our first record was in 1936. We was in Greenville, South Carolina, then. They'd heard about us. We hadn't been down in the Carolinas very long then. And I think they sent a man down from Charlotte to Greenville, South Carolina, to see if we would come and record, you know—for Victor records. We was playing shows then and we was drawing good crowds. But you know

29

you didn't charge much—fifteen for children and twenty-five for grown-ups. Playing schoolhouses and courthouses—I believe we was playing two programs a day when we was in Greenville. We played one in Charlotte of a morning,

The Original Bluegrass Boys: left to right: Art Wooten, Bill Monroe, Cleo Davis, Amos Garen *(Photo: courtesy, The Smithsonian Institution)*

Mr Gerard Bartholomew Kelly
101 Castle Road
Salisbury   SP1 3RP D.o.B.: 30 Dec 1946
Pharmacy: Rowlands DELIVERY   Age: 65 y
                                     NHS# 464 138 7133

REPEAT PRESCRIPTION WILL BE READY FOR COLLECTION WITHIN
48 HOURS
Surgery Website: www.stannstreetsurgery.co.uk
For PORTON ordering: prescriptions.porton@gp-j83020.nhs.uk
Dispensing patients to collect medicines from
St Ann Street Surgery [ ]
Porton [ ]
Winterslow Post Office [ ]
Winterbourne Shop [ ]
Whaddon shop [ ]
Coombe Bissett shop [ ]
Main Surgery ordering: prescriptions.stann@gp-j83020.nhs.uk
ST ANN STREET SURGERY NEW TELEPHONE NUMBER:
01722 342000 (START DATE: 24 NOVEMBER 2011)

Amlodipine 5mg tablets   [
tablets, take one daily
Last Issued: Thu 11 Oct 2012   Next Issue Due: Thu 08 Nov 2012
Issues Remaining: 5

Aspirin 75mg dispersible tablets   [
pack of 28 tablet(s), TAKE ONE DAILY to prevent heart disease
PLEASE ARRANGE TO SEE VANESSA IN THE HEART CHECK
CLINIC EVERY SEPTEMBER.
Last Issued: Tue 18 Sep 2012   Next Issue Due: Tue 16 Oct 2012
Issues Remaining: 4

Citalopram 20mg tablets   [
- tablet(s), take two daily for depression
Last Issued: Tue 18 Sep 2012   Next Issue Due: Tue 16 Oct 2012
Issues Remaining: 0

Nicholas Stanger
Ann Street Surgery
St. Ann Street
Salisbury   SP1 2PT
22342000

PATIENTS – please read the notes overleaf

Should you pay prescription charges? Read all the statements in **Part 1** opposite. You don't have to pay a prescription charge if any of the statements apply to you (the patient) on the day you are asked to pay. (A valid War Pension exemption certificate only entitles you to free prescriptions for your accepted disablement.) Put a cross in the first box in **Part 1** that applies to you, read the declaration and complete and sign **Part 3**.

Benefits which DO NOT provide exemption. You are NOT entitled to exemption from prescription charges because you receive Pension Credit Savings Credit, Incapacity Benefit, Disability Living Allowance, Contributions based Jobseeker's Allowance or Contributions based Employment and Support Allowance. Only those benefits listed in **Part 1** provide exemption. An HC3 certificate does not entitle you to free prescriptions.

Evidence. You may be asked to provide evidence to show that you do not have to pay. You could show the relevant benefit award notice, or an exemption or pre-payment certificate. If you cannot show evidence at that time you can still get your prescription items free but your Primary Care Trust will check your entitlement later if you do not show proof (see paragraph about Penalty Charges).

If you have to pay a prescription charge. You (or your representative) should put in **Part 2** the amount you have paid and then sign and complete **Part 3**.

Need help with the cost of prescription charges? You can get information by ringing 0845 850 1166 or by reading leaflets HC11 or HC12. You may be able t get these leaflets from your GP surgery or pharmacy. Or ring 0845 610 1112 to get one, or go to www.dh.gov.uk/helpwithhealthcosts

Not entitled to free prescriptions? Pre-pay to reduce the cost. If you think you will have to get more than 4 items in 3 months or 14 items in 12 months it wi be cheaper to buy a pre-payment certificate (PPC). Phone 0845 850 0030 to find out the cost, or order a PPC and pay by credit or debit card. You can pay for a 12 month PPC by direct debit instalment payments. Buy on-line at www.ppa.org.uk To pay by cheque get an application form (FP95) from your pharmacy or go to www.dh.gov.uk/helpwithhealthcosts The FP95 tells you what to do.

Do you need a refund? If you are unsure if you are entitled to free prescriptions you should pay for the prescription item(s) and ask for a receipt form FP57. **You must get the FP57 form when you pay for the item(s), you cannot get the form later.** If you find you didn't have to pay, you can claim your money back up to 3 months after paying. The FP57 form tells you what to do.

Patient Representative. If you are unable to collect your prescription yoursel someone can take your completed form for you. You must complete **Part 1**. Your representative must complete **Parts 2 and 3**. **Anyone who collects a Schedule 2 or 3 controlled drug must sign the box in Part 1 when they colle the item(s)** and provide proof of identity if requested.

Data collection. Information about the prescription items on this form will b processed centrally to pay monies due to the pharmacist, doctor or applianc contractor for the items they have supplied to you. The NHS will also use the information to analyse what has been prescribed and the cost. The Counter Fraud and Security Management Service, a division of the NHS Business Serv Authority, may use information from this form to prevent and detect fraud incorrectness in the NHS.

Penalty Charges. If it is found that you should have paid for your prescripti items, you will face penalty charges and may be prosecuted under the pow introduced by the Health Act 1999. Routine checks are carried out on exemption claims including some where proof may have been shown. You bb contacted in the course of such checks.

say at seven o'clock, then we'd drive to Greenville for a twelve. We had a
hundred miles to drive. Played two shows a day.
So we decided we would record, and I remember when we got to the
recording studios. It was kindly of a warehouse place where they had it. Just
where they kept their records and everything—their supply of records that
they sent out to different places. The Delmore Brothers was recording, and
Arthur Smith, and they stopped their session and let us take over and start
recording 'cause we just had a short time, you know, in order to get back and
play a show that night.

Their recordings enabled them to reach a greater audience, and the Monroe
Brothers soon became the phenomenon of the Carolinas.

"What Would You Give In Exchange For Your Soul?" was the first record
that was ever released. It was backed up by "This World Is Not My Home."
And it really sold good. It was a powerful hit in the Carolinas. We didn't make
much money out of it—maybe a cent-and-a-half a record—but it was in
depression days and us playing shows and having good crowds the depression
didn't hurt us after we got down in that part of the country, 'cause it was a lot
more money than we had ever made, you see. We really did have big crowds.
For a schoolhouse, we'd pack it twice or three times, or a courthouse, we'd
pack it, say, three times. And it didn't take much advertising. People listened
strictly to your program and you didn't have to put up much paper for your
advertising. We worked on a percentage with the schools. I believe they got 30
or 35 percent. And then after that was over with, why, we busted it down the
middle.
We would generally stay in a place a year-and-a-half, and then we would
move on to another town, you know; I think we moved from Greenville to
Raleigh, North Carolina, and stayed there a year-and-a-half or two years.

The move to Raleigh was the last move that Charlie and Bill made together.
They had been together steadily for six years, working hard and traveling a lot,
and somehow it seemed that there was always a little friction between them.

Bill was several years younger than Charlie and had always been treated as the young brother. He now felt that he had proved himself an equal. He was vigorous, competitive, and proud of the way he had come up. He heard music differently than Charlie. He kept hearing a bigger sound closer to the groups he had heard as a boy, with a fiddle in there along with the mandolin, guitar, and bass. He heard a stronger beat too, with more syncopation going against the beat, the way it happened in blues. Somehow what he and Charlie were doing, good as it was, and successful as it was, didn't satisfy Bill personally or musically. He had to get on his own.

If we'd have had a manager, you know, no telling how far we could have gone. But so many times brothers can't get along good, you know. One wants to be the boss and the other one's mad because he does and so it was just better that we split up. Monroe Brothers was great, but Bill Monroe and his Bluegrass Boys are greater. It's a different style from what the Monroe Brothers had. Monroe Brothers didn't have no beat, and the Bluegrass Boys have a beat to their music.
Took me about a month to get a new band together. I think I rehearsed every day for a month. To start with I was getting a singer and a guitar man. That's what I wanted to carry, you know—have some good singing. So that was the first thing that I done. I hired Cleo Davis. And then I got a fiddle player. Art Wooten was his name. And after I got that, the next man I hired, he played a jug, you know, it sounded like a bass. His name was John Miller, from Ashville. And he could play spoons and bones, you know, and could play good comedy—played blackface comedian. We was there in Ashville, North Carolina, three months after I got the Bluegrass Boys together. I had tried to work over in Little Rock, Arkansas, but it played out there so I came to Ashville. Then I moved to Greenville and the jug player stayed with us a short time, and then I got a bass man, Amos Garen. And we worked there, I guess, and went to Nashville and tried for the Grand Ole Opry and made it there.

The Grand Ole Opry had been going for about ten years when Bill joined it. The emphasis during its early years was on old-time music and comedy. It was

a blend of medicine show, minstrel show, and revival meeting. Uncle Dave
Macon, "The Dixie Dewdrop," set the style with his freewheeling, nonstop
delivery of jokes, old-time banjo tunes, and comic songs. His voice was tough
and leathery and needed no amplification. Uncle Dave's home was on a stage
in a tent with a thousand weatherbeaten faces in front of him creased with
smiles. Along with Uncle Dave went Sam and Kirk McGhee "from sunny
Tennessee," the Fruitjar Drinkers, and the Crook Brothers. The music was
old-time string-band music, flavored with some blues and novelty tunes. At the
time much comedy was done in blackface, and two of the most popular
minstrel comics were Jamup and Honey. Another early star on the Opry was
an exceptional harmonica player named Deford Bailey. He was the only
Negro ever to be a regular member of the Opry.
A year before Bill joined the Opry another new face appeared—a young fiddle
player and singer from Tennessee named Roy Acuff. He wasn't a great
fiddler, but his voice was unlike anyone else's—mournful, choked with emotion
—the first of the "heart" singers. When Bill arrived Roy Acuff was already
on his way to becoming a big star, but Bill's music was different from Acuff's
and he didn't worry. He also knew it was different from the old-timers on the
show, although it had its roots in old-time music. He knew that his "Bluegrass
Boys" were ready and that his music would make its mark.

When I started on the Grand Ole Opry, I had rehearsed and we was ready.
Our music was in good shape. We had a good fiddler with us—for bluegrass
in them days—Fiddlin' Art Wooten. And my singing was high and clear,
you know, and I was in good shape, and we was ready to go on the Grand
Ole Opry. Really the only competition we had there was Roy Acuff, and
they was two different styles altogether.
Charlie and I had a country beat I suppose, but the beat in my music—
bluegrass music—started when I ran across "Muleskinner Blues" and
started playing that. We don't do it the way Jimmy Rodgers sung it. It's
speeded up, and we moved it up to fit the fiddle and we have that straight
time with it, driving time. And then we went on and that same kind of time
would work with "John Henry" and we put it on that. And when we started
here on the Grand Ole Opry, "Muleskinner Blues" and "John Henry"
were the numbers we tried out with. And it was something different for

them, and they really wanted it. It's wonderful time, and the reason a lot of people like bluegrass is because of the timing of it.

And then we pitched the music up where it would do a number some good. If you play in B-natural and sing there and your fiddle is right up there playing where you're at and the banjo, well it just makes it a different music from where it would be played if it was just drug along in G, C, or D.

The old-time sound, if they was playing in A they played in Open A. They wouldn't note when they should have been noting, and that's where bluegrass has been a school to a lot of entertainers—or been a help to 'em. It's not only in bluegrass but in the country field too. It's been kindly like a teacher for so many country-music singers and the musicians to follow the ideas of bluegrass players if the bluegrass people could play right and was doing it right. And that's where bluegrass has helped country music. To me bluegrass is really the country music. It was meant for country people.

The country people certainly lost no time in letting Bill know their reaction to the new sound. When he finished playing his new version of the "Muleskinner Blues" for the first time on the Opry, the house came down.

I know when we started there that "Muleskinner" was the first number to ever get an encore there. Started getting so many that other numbers would get 'em too. They had to put a stop to it.

The other musicians on the Opry knew that here was a man to be reckoned with. Bill broke precedents right and left.

We was the first to ever wear a white shirt on the Opry or wear a tie. We was the first outfit to ever play in B-flat or B-natural and E. Before that it was all C, D, and G. Fiddle men had a fit and they wouldn't hardly tackle it and they'd swear that they wanted to play straight stuff and they figured that that's where I should sing. And that's where bluegrass really advanced music.

34

BOSSMAN BILL MONROE

The first quartet I sang on the Grand Ole Opry—back in them days I sang a high lead with a tenor under it and Tommy Magnus sang baritone and Cleo Davis sang bass. And we sung "Farther Along" and it was really good. There wasn't a quartet on the Grand Ole Opry before us.

Bill stopped the show every week with his high singing and jumping band. Every week thousands of people listening to their radios out in the country through Tennessee, Kentucky, Alabama, Mississippi, the Carolinas, and everywhere the Grand Ole Opry reached were struck by this new voice, this new style. Bill Monroe and his Bluegrass Boys were talked about over many a Sunday dinner in that fall of 1939. By the start of the new year the people running the Opry decided it was time to start booking Bill out to play shows.

We worked on the Grand Ole Opry about ten weeks before they would even try to book me. Our first date was out of Nashville about twenty-five or thirty miles. I remember we taken in forty-five or sixty-five dollars— somewhere in that neighborhood. But you was still getting a small admission fee. And then we started out playing in Alabama. Seemed like that was the first state seemed like we could draw good in. And then it went to spreading, you know, into West Virginia and Kentucky, and, of course, I held a good standard in the Carolinas. They remembered me there.

Within a year Victor decided that Bill had better do some recording to satisfy his growing numbers of fans. They did a couple of sessions over in Atlanta, and the new sound was successfully captured. It was live and exciting. "Muleskinner Blues" showed off Bill's yodeling and fancy guitar work. Bill's lead singer, Clyde Moody, sang a mellow "Six White Horses." "In The Pines" featured Bill's shivering tenor over Cousin Wilbur's lead. And Tommy Magnus's bluesy, country fiddling soared on "Katy Hill."

"Katy Hill" had more in it when we recorded than it had ever had before. Those old-time fiddlers didn't have nobody to shove them along. Now

Tommy Magnus had been playing with Roy Hall and they were trying to play off of bluegrass. He'd heard the way we played when Art Wooten was with me so it was right down his alley to get somebody behind him with that, because with that kind of little bow that he worked he could move you right along.

Successful as these recordings were—and they were big hits, selling tens of thousands in the South—Bill felt that he should change to another company. Charlie still recorded for Victor, and Bill wanted his music to be totally free of any shadow his older brother might cast. So he went to Columbia Records where he stayed until 1950.

For two years Bill had kept a four-piece band—fiddle, mandolin, guitar, and bass—but he was going to go on a tent show with Jamup and Honey and he thought that he could use another comedian in addition to his bass man. A banjo player/comedian named Stringbean (real name Dave Akeman) had written asking for work, so Bill hired him. The banjo gave the band a stronger tie to the old-time music Bill had heard as a boy, and the new addition suited his ear.

After the '41 season with Jamup and Honey, Bill was a big enough star to go out on his own with a tent.

I went out with a fellow named Bill Whalley from Miami, Florida. He furnished the tent and I furnished the music. Then the next year I bought a tent and I kept that tent for three or four years.

We had seven trucks and twenty-eight men working at first. We carried the tent, bleachers, chairs, electric light and power, and a cook house. Later we cut it down to seven men. They could set it up in two-and-a-half hours. And it didn't cost you a lot to put on a show in a town in those days. Sixty-five dollars tops would cover newspaper ads, window cards, the license, everything. I had a stretched out bus. I had a Chevrolet bus with four seats in it. I carried ten people that worked for me, hauled 'em with that bus. Sam and Kirk McGhee worked for me, and Deford Bailey worked a lot for me and Uncle Dave Macon.

Deford Bailey played a big part in the Grand Ole Opry years ago. He made a

many a mile with me. We rode together right in the back seat. Lots of times we would have trouble getting him lodgings. We'd walk the streets together, two, three o'clock in the morning, nobody out, in the roughest parts of town we'd be down there getting him a place to stay. We wore riding pants and hats back in them days, and I suppose they thought we was the law and nobody would ever bother us. Then he would get in the room and lock the door and stay there until I went to get him the next day.

He always wanted "that old ham sandwich"—that's what he called it. Country

All aboard! The Blue Grass Special, with a carload of Bluegrass Boys and Girls and a truckload of musical instruments, leaves the Opry House every Saturday midnight for big personal appearance shows.

left to right: Bill Monroe, Amos Garen, Stringbean, Lester Flatt, Mr. & Mrs. Howdy Forrester

ham it was, the highest one they had—thirty-five cents—and the rest of us could eat quarter sandwiches.

Uncle Dave was good to work with. He was a pretty smart man—had beautiful handwriting. He had never entertained until he was fifty-two years old. Before that he was a farmer. If the crowd was right he could handle it better than anyone you have ever seen go out there. But if they was down, he

absolutely couldn't do nothing with them. He couldn't get off the stage quick
enough. But if he had a big crowd there he'd say, "The old man can still get
them in." But if nobody was there then he'd say I wasn't doing so good.

With a tent Bill could go into any area, set the tent up, pack in two or three
thousand people a show, play two or three shows, and move on to the next area.
To people in the country the tent show was the biggest event of a season, and
Bill's rapidly became one of the most popular and successful shows of the time.
Monroe's shows had a fire and a punch that set them apart from the others.
To begin with, Uncle Dave and the McGhees were nonstop entertainers,
keeping up a steady stream of jokes, routines, comic songs, and instrumentals.
Deford Bailey was an extraordinary harmonica player who would break up
audiences with his "Fox Chase" solo. And then, with the audience well
warmed-up, out would stride Bill Monroe with his Bluegrass Boys. He wore
high riding boots, riding pants, and a black hat. He was a big man and he had
authority. Without a word the band would start playing, and the people
realized that here was someone who meant business. His singing was high and
clear as a bell, his mandolin cut through on solos and supplied a driving beat
behind the others, the fiddle would swing into its breaks like a frightened deer,
and when they all sang together on gospel numbers, the harmonies with Bill
way up on top gave people the shivers. This was not just another old-time
band. It was driving and together. It brought the audience up to a new level
of musical experience. They instinctively recognized a special musical
excellence that was part of their culture, that was theirs to share. They realized
that there was more to their music than a few laughs and a whoop. It said
something to them stronger and deeper than music had before. This new
mixture of lonesome, blue, old-time, jazzy, religious music hit country people
inside. Bill Monroe gave dignity and meaning to their music, and they
responded.
When Bill heard this response, he knew he was on the right track. In a way he
was just flying on instruments, relying on his instincts to guide him in the
best way to shape his new music and get the most out of the men with him.
Much of the music was in his head, stored up there from the days when he was
a boy. He used individuals in his band to help him get that music out. When
a man worked with Bill his playing invariably improved.

BOSSMAN BILL MONROE

With the ideas of other people, you know, a fiddler, a good singer, or a man who could play a good banjo, why I could use a lot of his ideas—you know I can hear them—and see what I want to use that he's got. But I remember times and things that I bring out each year that I've kept, you know, that accumulated back when I was really a kid, that I want to use through the life of the Bluegrass Boys while I'm with 'em. I believe in hunting for the high tones for bluegrass. And the clear, brilliant sound and good time, good drive to it. And if you've got a high note, why I believe in hitting that note, not try to dodge it or get around it. And I think that is a help to bluegrass. Be sure you have it in right time. If it's a waltz, don't try to play it in fox-trot time. If they're working for you and they're playing the numbers that I'd be singing—say we've got a good fiddler and we take on a banjo player that he hasn't done much of it—by the time he works with us a month he'll see that he didn't have it right, that he was on the wrong track. And he'll see that the style we are playing will be much better for him.

I have taken Gordon Terry when he could barely play three tunes and they wasn't on the money. He was hitting the notes sharp and flat. He'd always loved bluegrass, but he had never played it, you see. He'd played along with his brothers. Then when he got in bluegrass, to play it right, there's a skill to it —you've got to know how to handle that bow right and time it and use the right notes with bluegrass and then it will go to really getting good for you and paying off. Well, Gordon made into a good fiddler. Kenny Baker, you know, he played a swing fiddle and played for Don Gibson before he went to work for me. And I guess played a good fiddle. I never did hear him much. But I do know that he made a wonderful fiddle player after he got with us. And he learned bluegrass. And I think today that he'd rather play bluegrass than what he played years ago.

It don't only take a fiddle or the banjo; the guitar man, he's got to learn too. It's a style. A guitar means as much in a bluegrass band as anything else. And the bass man's got to carry his part too. Just like with the mandolin you've got to note with that little finger. It means so much to set that in there. Well, I learned that when I was a kid, you know, that that little finger would pay off for you if you would give it a chance. So it just takes a lot of learning and a lot of practice. It's a music that takes a lot of practice to play bluegrass right.

BOSSMAN BILL MONROE

And I think it's a music the more you play it, the more you like to play it, the more you like to hear yourself play it, and you know just how good you can play it—if you fool with it long enough. And you can see a feller that's coming up alongside of you over there that's playing a good banjo, playing a good fiddle, or mandolin, and you know he's gonna come on up and pass you if you don't stay in the collar.

As is always the case, great music has to have great men to play it, and Bill had the talent for picking the right men at the right time. His band became his instrument as much as the mandolin, and after five years Bill was really coming into his own as a leader. Things began to really fall into place in 1945. Bill hired Lester Flatt to play guitar and sing lead for him. Lester was about Bill's age, and he had worked with Charlie after Bill and Charlie had broken up. His voice was light and easy and it blended with Bill's better than anyone's had before.

When a singer comes with me, I've got to work on it to get our voices right. When Lester Flatt came with me, he was weak, you know. I couldn't hardly hear him sing beside of me. He would listen to me, how I would sing a song and how I would handle the words and he would learn kindly under that. And singing in quartets he'd know he'd have to get in there. I thought Lester made a good singer with me. Pretty fine.

After Lester had been with Bill for a while, a young banjo player who played in a new three-finger style was brought to Bill's attention. He was from over near Shelby, North Carolina, and his name was Earl Scruggs.

To start with, I wanted the five-string banjo touch and Stringbean was the only man around and then Earl Scruggs came along and gave it a real boost with that kind of banjo playing.

41

Earl Scruggs recalls how he came to work with Bill:

I worked in Knoxville for Lost John Miller. I was in a group that tried out for the show there. We didn't make it, but Lost John asked about the banjo player in the group, and I started working with him. Then he came to Nashville to start a Saturday morning program. We still lived in Knoxville and worked there and we would come over to Nashville to do the Saturday show. I was friends with Jimmy Shumate who worked with Bill then (the band included Lester Flatt, Birch, Jim Andrews on tenor banjo and comedy, Shumate, and Bill). Each Saturday Jimmy would want me to quit Lost John and go with Bill. Then towards the end of 1945 Lost John disbanded, and I told Shumate that I was out of a job and would probably go back home so he set it up for Bill to listen to me. Bill came over to the Tulane Hotel and listened to a couple of tunes. He didn't show much reaction, but he asked me to come down to the Opry and jam some. He showed interest, but I think he wasn't sure exactly of the limits of it or how well it would fit his music, but he asked me if I could go to work on Monday and I said "Yes."

Soon after Earl Scruggs joined the band, a fiddler from Florida named Chubby Wise, who had been with Bill earlier, rejoined the band.

Art Wooten started, then Tommy Magnus, then Art came back, then Big Howdy Forrester came and worked on up until he had to go into service, then Tommy came back in '43. Then Chubby Wise came up looking for a job one Saturday night and he wanted to try out. He'd been in a swing band and he just couldn't fiddle. He was fighting it to get it like Howdy had it. Howdy played some pretty bluegrass music. "Footprints in the Snow," he really played it pretty.

But Bill had challenged Chubby, and he was determined to "fight it" until he had it. It might have had something to do with the Spanish blood in him, but Chubby was to become one of the most soulful fiddle players bluegrass was to see. He would put in a lot of blues licks and he had a sweet tone that meshed beautifully with Lester and Bill when they sang.

This particular band, which included Lester, Earl, and Chubby, with Bill's brother Birch on bass, set the style for bluegrass bands to come. "Blue Moon of Kentucky," "Molly and Tenbrooks," "Mother's Only Sleeping," "Wicked Path of Sin," "I'm Going Back to Old Kentucky," "Bluegrass Breakdown," and many others that the group recorded for Columbia at the time became the classics of bluegrass music.

It was an exciting time to be with Bill, but it was not easy. He was always pushing a man, trying to get more out of him, testing him. This went for everything, not just music. The weeks were the seven-day kind, the pay little, and sleep generally accomplished while sitting up in the car on the way to another show. Yet through it all was a togetherness and a spirit generated by the music they found themselves playing.

It was a memorable time for Earl Scruggs.

Back then the term "sideman" wasn't used as it is today. It was a leader and his group and you all worked together. It was hard work but we had a lot of fun. I loved Bill like a brother and he was always good to me. He took great interest in the work he was doing, and I felt appreciated. He was high on my list as a musician, and he had a solid beat that could support anything you wanted to pick. He would spend a lot of time just tightening up the group. Some rehearsals we wouldn't sing a song. We would just concentrate on the sound of the band.

We were working all the time. Sometimes we wouldn't see a bed from one end of the week till the other. In theaters we would do four or five or six shows a day from eleven in the morning until eleven at night. Sometimes we would do what was called "bicycling"—we would play a show in a theater— then while the movie was on go play in another theater and come back to the first one while the movie was on in the second.

It was a must then to make it back to the Opry on Saturday night. Sometimes if we were over on the East Coast somewhere, it was all we could do to make it back. But the Opry meant so much to the people then in the towns. When

I was at home people who didn't have a radio would go to a neighbor's and they would all sit around listening to the Opry. So we would never miss it no matter where we had to come from.

It was hard traveling then on bad roads in a stretched-out car with no place

Bill Monroe, Chubby Wise, Birch Monroe, Lester Flatt, Earl Scruggs

to lie down. Sometimes you'd feel so bad and fall asleep and then wake up and someone would maybe tell a story and we'd laugh and feel good again. But Bill would never let the music go down no matter how tired we were. If a man would slack off, he would move over and get that mandolin close up on him and get him back up there. He would shove you and you would shove him and you would really get on it.

We played in rain, we played in snow, we played where the power would go off and we would have to play by lantern light with no sound. We had two bad wrecks, but nobody got hurt. The way we had to drive to make dates it's a wonder we weren't killed. But we made it, and it toughened us up to encounter and overcome these difficulties. It seemed to make Bill stronger and it brought out the deep feeling and love he had for what he was doing.

This sense of togetherness was shared by Bill.

Working with a lot of the boys down through the years I've tried to help them and see that they played their part right. A lot of them have played their part well and you wouldn't have to help them too much. But there's been many young kids that have started to work with me that I have really taken a lot of pains with and when he got to where he could carry his part with the fiddle or banjo or singing and the guitar man was coming in there and you had a good bass man, it just made it into a good combination together, and it was everybody pulling for the same thing in the way of a band and it was like one for all and all for one.

I don't like to impose on nobody. I think they should see things that need to be done, you know. Just like in music—if I can help anybody, why I want to do it. I don't mean to make them think "Well, hell, you think you're the smartest thing that ever walked." That ain't it. If I can help, I want to. And he might have things that might help me, but I study them, you know, and I'll never take something from him that he'll ever find. If I've taken a note from anyone, why I wouldn't take it to steal it, or use all of his note. I might get the idea or something and work it into the mandolin. But there's been many a note put on the banjo from the mandolin. Earl's taken note after note. And there's fiddlers that play the way I think it should be played, and it's a big help to bluegrass music, I think, to know how to set that note right in there, you know, and let it be separated from the other note, and not let one note hurt the other one. I've tried to be a leader, you know, not a boss.

Bill Monroe, Earl Scruggs, Birch Monroe, Lester Flatt

I never did like to try to boss somebody and give him a hard time to go, without he's lazy as a dog. If he's too lazy or hard to get out of bed, well, we'll have trouble. And I just can't go along. And I don't like a drunk, you know. I can't take anybody that something else means more than his music, if his music is his living. Though I'll go along with him some. I think anybody ought to see things that ought to be done.

Probably the most significant change in the bluegrass sound occurred at this time. The banjo now came up to the fiddle and the mandolin as a lead instrument. The three-finger picking style that Earl Scruggs had been developing was an extension of the old-time two-finger picking style. Others were working in the same direction—Snuffy Jenkins for one, Don Reno for another. The difference was that Earl joined Monroe and Bill began to feature Earl on every show. The new sound was heard by thousands who couldn't believe that so many notes could be played on a banjo so smoothly. The audience tore the roof off the Opry House. It was a new experience for Earl.

I had heard Snuffy Jenkins play with a three-finger roll and my older brother did some, but when I started here no one had heard the style before and people would gather around me like I was a freak almost. Bill started featuring Banjo tunes like "Molly and Tenbrooks" and "Whitehouse Blues," and he wrote "Bluegrass Breakdown" to feature the banjo and I had "Dear Old Dixie" worked out. Some of these tunes started catching on and he started featuring me pretty heavy and I appreciated it.

The singing was better than ever, too. Lester and Bill blended together like honey and butter. On songs like "Summertime Has Passed and Gone" or "Mother's Only Sleeping," Lester's voice could be soft and wistful, evoking past memories seen through a twilight haze. On fast numbers like "Lovin' Another Man" or "I'm Going Back to Old Kentucky," his voice had a smoky, light quality as it skimmed over the top of the melody, swooping low here and high there. And wherever Lester was, Bill was on top, singing effortlessly even in falsetto.

The best singing that the group did was on hymns, which Bill felt strongly about. Some were traditional, others he wrote, and all were done with precision and care. Bill's brother Birch sang bass at the time, Earl sang baritone, Lester lead, and Bill tenor. But Lester's voice was pitched at tenor range, so Bill was actually singing high tenor. The hymns were generally complex, involving various patterns of leads and repeats, with solo passages for the bass and high tenor as well as the lead. Between verses, Bill would insert a brilliant mandolin break. Before the Bluegrass Quartet there had been no singing of this kind on the Opry, and no other group ever could match Bill's group at doing this material. Hymns were the solid base of his music.

That's the main thing, I think. To let the people know that you believe in what you're doing. That it's true. On gospel songs some people didn't see how I could come up with such good titles—as wicked as I was, was the words they put it. And people talking, you know, they really didn't know. You can't judge people like that. I don't think I'd be as wicked as people who drinked and gambled and smoked and fought every day. As far as being wicked, I don't think that I would be any more wicked probably than they was who'd even mention this stuff, see? It was Charlie and his wife was the ones that was talking about it. And many, many people have told me that my songs changed them. And it's not only hymns that moves people. There's a lot of bluegrass that moves you too. Might not move you in that way, but they still move you. In fact a lot of 'em still moves me—or other people that can really sing a good song.

At the same time that Bill's music was coming together so well in the forms he was working out with his group, the music and style of the Opry was changing and developing too. It was becoming less a music show and more one of personalities. Roy Acuff had been joined by Red Foley, Pee Wee King and the Golden West Cowboys featuring Eddy Arnold, and Ernest Tubb. Acuff and Tubb took care of the heart songs and laments while King, Foley, and Arnold were smooth singers with a more modern approach. Most of the groups used electric and Hawaiian steel guitars. During the war years, the audience for "hillbilly" music had greatly expanded, and the music was becoming more contemporary. The postwar years saw another major influx of country people into urban areas looking for factory work. Honky-tonks and wild, wild women were becoming major subjects for songs. The stars of the Opry took a cue from the cowboys in the movies and started wearing elaborate cowboy outfits and driving Cadillacs, the perfect fulfillment of their fans' dreams of success, fame, and fortune that had driven them to leave the farm behind. The old days of Uncle Dave, the McGhees, and Deford Bailey were becoming a dim memory blotted out by the spangles and electric guitars.

Despite this trend, Bill Monroe concentrated on his music, honing it, polishing it, weaving the various strands of his musical background into a new and exciting pattern. Instead of escaping from his past, he was taking everything that he valued in it and reworking it for the only people he cared about—the country people. It was for them that he played, and they understood it and appreciated it. Bill made their music seem more alive and brilliant than it had ever been before. Country people sensed that this was the best they would ever be, and they would pack the tent or the hall or the schoolhouse, roaring their approval of Earl's new way with the banjo, shaking their heads at Chubby's bluesy fiddle work, soaking up Lester's easy vocals, calling out to Bill to do "Muleskinner" or a "Blue Yodel," and letting out a whoop when he would bear down and really put it to the rest of the boys on "John Henry." For these people Bill Monroe's music was the true soul of the Opry. He got to them like nobody else, and his awareness of this gave him the energy and strength to continue developing his music the way he knew it must go—regardless of the fashions of the moment on the Opry.

If I had got up there and sang everything solos with a little fiddle music behind me or a guitar like Ernest Tubb does, it would have got awful old. But with everybody where they could play their parts good and carrying a quartet or a trio or duet and letting the guitar man sing some solos, it made it good. There's more to it than just one man singing.

If a man listening will let it, bluegrass will transmit right into your heart. If you love music and you listen close, it will come right on into you. If that fiddle's cutting good and they're playing pretty harmonies it will make cold chills run over me and I've heard it many times. If you really love bluegrass music it will dig in a long ways. If you take time to listen close to the words and the melody it will do something for you.

Every band leader has one continuing problem: personnel. Bill almost forgot about it in the successful years following the war. It almost seemed as if his worries were over. He had finally found the right men for his music, his records were successful, he was working nearly every day in the year, and he had done it his own way. He had set new musical standards for the Opry and established himself as a major figure despite his refusal to follow the current trends. But things never stand still for long in music, and in 1948 Bill was hit by the problem he had almost forgotten about.

Earl was the first to go. He was reluctant to do so because playing with Bill had been a happy experience for him. When he went with Bill, he was young, still working up his style on the banjo. Bill had been good to him, almost like an older brother, and his banjo playing had really matured and defined itself under the influence of Bill's music. If music had been the only thing in his life, Earl probably would have stayed, but he had a commitment to his family back in North Carolina, and he felt that he had to go where he was needed to help support them, probably by going to work in a factory.

Bill hardly had a chance to miss Earl, though. Another banjo picker had been waiting for this moment since 1943. Don Reno had played for Bill then, and would have joined him if he hadn't had to go into the service. When he heard that Earl was leaving, he was on his way.

Bill came through Spartanburg in the fall of forty-three. Chubby Wise hadn't been long with him. Sam and Kirk McGhee were with him and Chubby was learning breakdowns from Floyd Ethridge. And we stayed in the Franklin Hotel in Spartanburg and played all day. They hadn't never heard

my style of banjo playing before, I don't reckon. And they got me started
playing and I played all day over there. I was playing "Sally Goodwin,"
"Lonesome Road Blues," "Sally Johnson," "Bully of the Town."
Bill came in a little after noon and he stayed three hours playing. In fact we
had the band going—Chubby Wise and him and Clyde Moody and Cousin
Wilbur and myself. The sound was a little rough then because it hadn't
been smoothed down. But it was the same sound that he later on had. And
he told Clyde that day, "This is the sound right here that I want."
Bill offered me a job. I told him I was going to volunteer for the service and
if I didn't pass I would come to work for him, but I passed and went into
the service. In the meantime Scruggs went to work for Bill.
When I heard that Scruggs was leaving, I went to Nashville and Bill was
gone to North Carolina, so I doubled back and went to the theater in
Taylorsville where he was playing. He had no banjo player with him so I
got my banjo out, tuned up, and walked out on the stage and started playing
with him. Lester was with him and Bill gave me one of the hardest rows to
hoe that night I ever seen. He started playing everything in B-flat or
B-natural because I didn't have a capo and he was getting a kick out of
watching me. He was nudging Lester and getting a kick out of it.
So we went to Mt. Airy, North Carolina, and played some radio shows with
him and a stage show. And he took me to a cafe and said, "I don't know
how much you're used to making." I said that money wasn't the thing. I
didn't care what he was paying. He was paying ninety dollars a week and
fifteen dollars extra on Sundays.

Shortly after Don arrived, Lester, too, decided that it was time to go. He
felt that he could do as well, or better, on his own, and he handed in his
notice. Bill wasn't happy about it.

Now I didn't care to see Lester go. I'd have liked for him to stay on. Being
as he wanted to go, why I accepted his notice. And then he wanted to go

ahead and work, you know, 'cause he would've except nobody didn't ask
him to.

You put a lot of time into bringing someone along. Taking him when he
wasn't very much, you know. And I guess they really don't think. They

Birch Monroe, Don Reno, Bill Monroe, Mac Wiseman, Joel Price

think, you know, "Well I'll be with him as long as he wants me," but then
they get up and they learn to sing, you know, and they think "Well no,
I'd better get out on my own if I'm going to do anything." So then it really
hurts the man that you've been with. He has to start all over and get

another man. And they think that they're going to have it easy, but they find it a lot harder when they start than they think it's going to be.

Losing Earl Scruggs and Lester Flatt within such a short time didn't make Bill happy, but it was a fact of life that he as a bandleader could learn to live with. For the moment, Reno sang some lead and played guitar as well as banjo. Then a smooth singer named Jim Eanes came in to sing lead. Then Don persuaded Bill to give a young singer from Virginia, Mac Wiseman, a chance at it. He had a strong, rich voice, and he stayed with Bill long enough to make some memorable recordings, notably, "Sweetheart of Mine, Can't You Hear Me Calling."

Looking back, it seems that hardly a beat was missed between the time Lester and Earl left, and new men came in to take their place. It was no accident. Bill's music had reached out all over the South, and there were hundreds of young singers and fiddlers and banjo players who were getting together to play his music and their own. The best of them had an ambition: that someday they would be able to play with Bill as a Bluegrass Boy. The music had become crystalized into a style that could be imitated and developed by others even if they couldn't all play with Bill. Bluegrass music —as it was coming to be called—was starting to have a life of its own. Bill was its sun and source of energy and inspiration. Before long there were to be many satellite bands following their own individual orbits.

After leaving Bill, Lester Flatt had gone to Raleigh, North Carolina, where he started with a radio show of his own. He asked Earl if he would want to play with him there and at any shows they could get in the area. Earl agreed as long as it wouldn't take him away from home too much, and soon they had a group under the name of Lester Flatt, Earl Scruggs and the Foggy Mountain Boys. Up in Virginia, Carter and Ralph Stanley were utilizing their own heritage as a basis for their own unique style of old-time bluegrass. By 1950 Don Reno had left Bill to join with Tommy Magnus and Red Smiley in a group, and Mac Wiseman made his way back to Virginia to begin his career on his own. Don Reno was replaced by another young banjo player named Rudy Lyle, and Bill came up with a strong lead singer, Jimmy Martin.

The way talent kept coming into the band and then spinning out on its own

seems organic and right. At the time, Bill was almost too busy to notice
what was happening. All he knew was that he was as busy as a man could be,
and that he couldn't lose too much sleep over men leaving. He had shows to
play. People were always coming up to him asking to join his band. He
didn't really have to go looking for replacements. Bill always seemed to wind
up with the right men at the right time. He had an eye for potential and
had learned how best to bring a new man along.

One reason I guess a lot of people didn't stay too long back then was it was a
hard life. You had shows to play then and radio programs. You couldn't sit
down. You had to keep going and if a man booked you seven days in a row,
you had to make them. To my way of believing you can't back out on
anything—if you've got some work to do, do it.
One thing about my music is that this hasn't hurt me too bad because each
man would give me different ideas and different stuff to work from that he
probably didn't realize that I was using or that was helping. Though he'd
had it in his mind, probably, to leave in three years or less, as soon as he
could do something. A lot of 'em didn't hurt.
And then down through the years you keep changing. You keep getting
young boys coming with you and wanting to learn, and when they get past
that learning they really get good right there. And some of them can hold it
right there and some of them can't and they want to go on out and get better.
And while they're really learning and coming along fine that's when they
really make a good bluegrass man.

On this point Don Reno agreed:

As far as being a good bandmaster, I think he's one of the best I ever worked
with. He never would lose his temper. If you wasn't playing a tune the way
he wanted you to play it, he'd keep playing it until you got it, and he'd
look at you with kind-of-a-half grin on his face, you know, when you got it
right. He made you get it for yourself.

Bill Monroe on his horse, King Wilkie

He knew whether or not you could make it. And he'd set up a bank on each side of you and drive you right down the middle.

Despite his breakneck pace, Bill began to find time to indulge his other interests. He had bought a large farm outside of Nashville and began to raise Tennessee walking horses. They were beautiful animals, and he had a keen appreciation of their style and poise. Many other stars of the day in Nashville also raised horses, but they seemed to be imitating a Hollywood notion of cowboy life. Bill tempered the cowboy with his Kentuckian's sense of good horsemanship and breeding.

Another interest that Bill brought with him from Kentucky was game chickens. He and Birch raised them, and whenever they had a chance they would put them up against all comers. It's an ancient and bloody sport that has lost its respectability in modern times, but Bill always liked to watch a particularly game chicken overcome a bigger opponent. Aside from the gambling part, the sport said something to him about heart and determination that he could relate to his own struggle to be the best.

Bill's most consuming preoccupation at this time was baseball. He decided that the only way to keep baseball from interfering with his music was to bring it along with him wherever he went.

I'd have liked to be a baseball player. I love baseball. But you have to have good eyes to play baseball and my eyes never was good. I could hit good and could've been a fair player.

In the late forties I had two ballclubs—one that traveled and one that worked out of Nashville. They were good ballclubs. Had college boys and ballplayers I picked up out of Nashville. The road club was called "The Bluegrass All-Stars," and the one out of Nashville was called "The Bluegrass Ballclub." I paid each man ten dollars a day and five or ten dollars if they hit a home run. And later on I paid the pitchers twenty or thirty dollars a day —if he was a good pitcher. Back when Happy Chandler was Commissioner there was plenty of ballclubs through the country and they was all working hard to get as far in it as they could get. And wasn't no trouble to get a game in any city. The club I had on the road I don't think was beat but only a couple or three times all season. They was really a wonderful club. There was a couple of teams in Kentucky and West Virginia that beat 'em. And the umpire beat 'em one place in Kentucky and one place in West Virginia.

You know, you can't beat an umpire. The clubs I had, you know, there was a lot of betting going on, you know. Some of the boys they'd bet—I didn't know it 'til later—that we'd score in the first inning. I had a man that could

Birch Monroe, Bill Monroe

get on base and I had another feller that could advance him, you know. If he could get him as far as third, he could steal home. He stole home many a time.

Stringbean played on the club on the road. He could play nearly any position. Then we had Jackie Phelps. He was a good shortstop and in the run of a season he'd only struck out three times. You couldn't hardly get him out. Then we had G. W. Wilkerson, he was a good singer. So we had some pretty good musicians in the club.

Back in them days if you was on the Grand Ole Opry you was rated pretty high, you know. Or if you worked for some group that was well known. So on the road we had the Shenandoah Valley Trio—they recorded some. Joel Price and G. W. Wilkerson was in it. Maybe Jimmy Martin sung tenor in that trio on some stuff. And Jackie Phelps was in it. We had two or three men to back them up.

When we came to town the ballclub would get out early and practice up until about seven-thirty and then the show would go on and it would go on for about half an hour before the game would start. And the game would start at eight o'clock.

We had some good names in our ballclub. We had Jim Kirby who played for the Cubs—he played center field for us. And we had a fellow by the name of Mac Faron who played for the Cotton Belt in Arkansas. And a catcher named Allen who caught for Bluefield, West Virginia, in the Appalachian League. We had pitchers who were scouted by Pittsburgh and the St. Louis Cardinals. I know we played Mt. Sterling, Kentucky, and this pitcher that we had struck out sixteen in a row. He was mowing 'em down. We taken on the best team in the eastern part of Kentucky which was Pikeville. We played seven innings and it was five and two in our favor.

Money was plentiful right in that spot and I remember there was eleven fifty-dollar bills that come into the show that night. 'Course there was a lot of silver dollars and two dollar bills in that part of the country.

We played about six games a week. Saturdays I would have to go into Nashville to play the Opry. But if the Shenandoah Valley Trio was out and there was enough show, then they would go right ahead and play seven days a week. Wasn't no trouble to get plenty of bookings. We taken the club through the Carolinas, Kentucky, West Virginia, Virginia, Louisiana,

BOSSMAN BILL MONROE

Mississippi, Missouri, Illinois. You made a lot of money. 'Course it cost a lot of money. I carried thirteen or fourteen players at ten dollars a man, besides the musicians. But you could play any little town. I worked a season, and the smallest crowd I had was four hundred and eighty dollars. It run from there on up to three thousand dollars a night—up in that bracket. I would average between fourteen and eighteen hundred dollars a night. If it was two or three hundred, I never would even count the money if it was that low—just carry on to the next town.

For those working with Bill then, like Don Reno, it was an exhilarating, if exhausting, time.

At this time Bill was making a lot of money. We worked every day almost and he drew big crowds. He came out with the first songbook. The first order was a boxcar full of books. We went down to the depot and hauled them out to his barn and in no time they were gone. We did an hour show on WSM at night and by mail he sold almost all of them.
'Course he had the tent show in the summer. We couldn't keep a crew together, and me and Joel Price and Bill put the tent up and took it down more than anybody else did. Bill loved to work. Nobody could work him down.
Traveling with that thing was out of this world. We had a forty-six Packard limousine and some of us rode in that limousine with our instruments and suitcases on top and in the trunk. Me and Joel Price did most of the driving. I'd drive to keep my legs stretched out.
Bill was more interested in ball than he was music at this time. I reckon this was a way of resting his mind from music. But he liked to kill me playing ball. We would work a show one night and drive to the next town and usually get in at an early morning hour and he'd have a ball game set up by ten o'clock with the local team.

The mixture of bluegrass and baseball was no stunt in Bill's eyes. He didn't

see it that way. To him music was a form of competition just like sports. It was a good way for a man to prove himself against other men. It was healthy. It kept you in shape and alert. His philosophy of life was embodied in everything he did, whether it was raising horses, fighting chickens, playing ball, or making music.

All the way through, bluegrass is competition with each man trying to play the best he can, be on his toes. You'll find it in every group. You'll find it in one group and another group following him. It works that way. They'll still be friends, but they'll work hard to be better than the other.

It seemed that the more Bill worked and traveled and played, the more music came out of him. He would sit up in the car fooling with his mandolin, watching the country go by, humming some tune, shaping some song in his head.

I think you really have to love music to travel. You know I love to travel. Seems like they went together with me. Some of my numbers it's helped and played a big part. Like "When The Golden Leaves Begin To Fall." That was right in autumn time, you know, and the leaves and everything were turning and the forest and the mountains and everything was really pretty, and, you know, winter would be coming soon—and I believe Mac Wiseman was with me back in those days—and seems like the song mighty near wrote itself after it got started.

> *Winter time is so cold in the mountains,*
> *The ground will soon be covered white with snow.*
> *How I long to keep the home fires burning,*
> *For I know my darling needs me so.*
>
> CHORUS: *When the moon shines on the Blue Ridge Mountains*
> *And it seems I can hear my sweetheart call,*

Photo: Carl Fleischhauer

How I long to be near my darlin',
*When the golden leaves start to fall.**

Other songs come out of my imagination. The song "The Little Girl and The Dreadful Snake," you know, I could imagine that. I could picture a family

with a little girl, and I know there's been stories like that down through the
years. There's somebody that had a little girl that got in bad.

> *Our darlin' wandered far away while she was out at play,*
> *Lost in the woods, she couldn't hear a sound,*
> *She was our darlin' girl, the sweetest girl in all the world,*
> *We searched for her but she couldn't be found.*

JAMES ROONEY

CHORUS: *I heard the screams of our little girl far away,*
Hurry, daddy, there's an awful, dreadful snake.
I ran as fast as I could through the dark and dreary wood,
But I reached our little girl too late.*

Then again, Bill was never reluctant to put the events of his own life into song. Some crystalized around the life he had left behind in Kentucky, the best being a tribute to his Uncle Pen.

Oh, the people would come from far away,
They'd dance all night till the break of day,
When the caller hollered "Do-Se-Do",
You knew Uncle Pen was ready to go.

CHORUS: *Late in the evening, about sundown,*
High on the hill and above the town,
Uncle Pen played the fiddle, oh how it would ring,
You could hear it talk, you could hear it sing.

He'd play an old piece called Soldier's Joy,
And then one called the Boston Boy,
But the greatest of all was Jenny Lynn,
To me that's where fiddlin' begins.

I'll never forget that mournful day
When Uncle Pen was called away.
They hung up his fiddle, hung up his bow,
They knew it was time for him to go.†

* "The Little Girl and The Dreadful Snake" *by Albert Price* ©1953 Tannen Music Inc. *Used with permission of the publisher; all rights reserved.*

† "Uncle Pen"—*Words and music by Bill Monroe. Copyright* ©1951 *by Hill and Range Songs, Inc. Used by permission.*

64

BOSSMAN BILL MONROE

You take somebody like Uncle Pen. I think it's a wonderful thing to write a song about him and to sing it. I don't think I would have done right if I didn't write a song about him. I think it's a wonderful thing.

During the early fifties, Bill very often used his songs as personal declarations. His heart songs differed from most in that they were true. Like all of his music, he put himself into it.

> *Traveling down this long, lonesome highway,*
> *I'm so lonesome I could cry.*
> *Memories of how we once loved each other.*
> *And now you are saying goodbye.*

CHORUS: *On and on I've followed my darlin'*
> *And I wonder where she can be.*
> *On and on I've followed my darlin'*
> *And I wonder if she ever thinks of me*

> *I've cried and cried for you little darlin',*
> *It breaks my heart to hear your name.*
> *My friends they also love you my darlin',*
> *And they think that I am to blame.*

> *I have to follow you little darlin'*
> *I can't sleep when the sun goes down.*
> *By your side is my destination,*
> *The road is clear, and that's where I'm bound.**

During much of this time, Jimmy Martin was singing lead with Bill. Jimmy came from Tennessee, and, like Bill, had absorbed much of the music he

---

65

heard around him as a youngster. He had an uncle who used to lead the singing in church, and Jimmy's own singing had an old-time flavor to it. He would come up on the end of a line, and when Bill and he sang together in fifths, both sliding up to their notes together, it was a lonesome and beautiful sound. Bill wrote many songs that made use of this sound while Jimmy was with him. Some of the most powerful were the gospel songs and hymns, like "The River of Death."

> *Oh the river of death (Oh the river of death)*
> *Lies just before me (Lies just before me)*
> *Can I find a place (Can I find a place)*
> *Where I can cross (Where I can cross)*
> *Or will I be (Or will I be)*
> *In sin forever (In sin forever)*
> *Oh Lord don't let (Oh Lord don't let)*
> *My soul be lost.*

CHORUS: *O I want to walk (Oh I want to walk)*
> *With Christ my Saviour (With Christ my Saviour)*
> *For he's the one (For he's the one)*
> *That'll guide me on (That'll guide me on)*
> *All through my life (All through my life)*
> *I've been a sinner (I've been a sinner)*
> *Now I'm right with God (Now I'm right with God)*
> *So I'm traveling home.**

Many times Bill could turn an accident or chance occurence to advantage. A major change in his sound, the use of twin fiddles, came about very casually.

I heard twin fiddles years ago, I guess, maybe in Bob Wills Band or—there was a group out of Atlanta that had twin fiddles—and Clayton McMichen

* "River of Death"— *Words and music by Bill Monroe. Copyright © 1951 by Hill and Range Songs, Inc. Used by permission.*

had twin fiddles back years ago in the twenties. It happened that I was on the Grand Ole Opry one night, you know, and there was these two fiddlers—one of them came in and he didn't even work with me—and they started playing twin fiddles and it sounded so good on numbers like "My Little Georgia Rose" that I decided that I would use some twin fiddle on some

left to right: Bill Monroe, Rudy Lyle, Joel Price, Jimmy Martin

stuff, and then other people around the Opry went to featuring it right quick because it was pretty and good.

Once he heard it, the twin fiddle sound really captured Bill's imagination.

He proceeded to write several tunes that captured the sound he heard in his head. They were all driving, fast-tempoed numbers which alternated sections of low-pitched intricate melodic lines with stretched-out, soaring, high harmony sections. It didn't seem to matter where he was or how he felt. They just came out.

When I wrote "Roanoke" I had the toothache the worst anybody had ever in this world. Everybody had gone out of the theater there in Roanoke but me and I felt so bad and I started playing and that's what I came up with. "Big Mon" was written in South Dakota. We was playing a square dance out there and it was wrote on the stage.

These tunes seemed to be ready made for the fiddlers that Bill was attracting to himself. There were many—Charlie Cline, Vassar Clements, Gordon Terry, Bobby Hicks, Red Taylor. Some songs were even recorded with three fiddles—"Tall Timber" and "My Little Georgia Rose." One fiddler who was knocked out by this new sound was Kenny Baker, who was to be associated with Bill for over fifteen years.

I played swing fiddle until I heard "Roanoke" and "Wheelhorse." The first time I ever heard "Roanoke," I thought it was the prettiest piece of music I'd ever heard. I'll bet you I put three dollars worth of damn nickels in that jukebox in Knoxville.
I was working in Knoxville, Tennessee, and I saw Bill just shortly after the releases on them and he talked to me about coming to work for him. I definitely couldn't play no bluegrass then. So I had to change my way of playing all around and really get after it. Take "Blue Moon of Kentucky"— that was very popular. I knew the melody and I could slightly play that. But you take "Muleskinner," "Foot Prints in the Snow"—that was another popular number, but I'd never fooled with it and I really had to hustle to work them out.
I worked with Bill fifty-six or fifty-seven the first time for a couple of years,

then sixty for a short time, then sixty-two until May of sixty-three and this last spell for a couple of years.

It's a hard way to make a living, but I enjoy it most of the time if everything goes good. And everyone is playing their parts well. It's a big enjoyment to me.

There's no more music in the world that you can play like bluegrass music. Particularly the fiddle. I've always found that you can play more from what you feel than any set pattern that most music is. In bluegrass you've got the melody to go by, but you play more or less what you feel. With someone like Don Gibson or any other modern country singer you knew exactly what lines you were going to play and all. That's the difference. In bluegrass you're more on your own. The tempos differ in bluegrass. A lot of times the same number will be played in different tempos. Depending on how you feel when you go into it, I suppose. Bill will kick off some numbers you know. One day he'll have a pretty good pace on it; the next day he'll have it a little bit slower. He never does the same number twice alike. There's always some change in that number every time he does it. I've always said that bluegrass music is nothing but a hillbilly version of jazz.

He'll let a man work a long time and see if he does have possibilities and the ability to adopt his way of playing. It was five or six months before he even undertook to show me an old number.

There's a lot of mechanical music being played today, and bluegrass is definitely not mechanical. It's strictly a heartfelt music; it's gotta be. You gotta like it to play it, because money-wise there's no living to be made for no sideman out of it. Some people love to live in the country just so they can exist from day to day. That's just like a bluegrass sideman. If he loves his music he can stay with it; if he don't—there you go.

Although Bill's music was deepening and growing, there were trends in the music world that were making it increasingly difficult for him to continue as he had for the past fifteen years as a successful bandleader.

A major breakthrough occurred in country music in 1952 and 1953 when a number of "pop" stars discovered and recorded some of Hank Williams's songs. The success of his music had been phenomenal enough before that,

Kenny Baker *(Photo: David Gahr)*

but it had been limited to the country market. "Your Cheatin' Heart" and "Cold, Cold Heart" showed the music world that the "hillbilly" music they had looked down on in the past could be a gold mine. There were many in Nashville who had long resented their "country cousin" image and were only too ready to move country music out toward a more urban and suburban sophisticated audience. One of the first to move "uptown" was

Eddy Arnold, "The Tennessee Ploughboy." Eddy left his plough behind and joined Patti Page, Dinah Shore, and Perry Como as a television performer. Another man who was ready to leave the country behind was Chet Atkins. He began to develop for RCA Victor the "Nashville Sound," which included string sections, choruses, and horns. Perhaps more than any other man, Atkins moved Nashville to becoming a recording center rivaling New York. The only price was a good chunk of the soul of country music. While this was going on, there was another development that was a challenge to Nashville and to country music. It originated in Memphis in response to the national breakout of rhythm and blues or, as it was later known, rock and roll. The music from Memphis was called rock-a-billy. There were several singers, including Jerry Lee Lewis, Carl Perkins, Johnny Cash, and Roy Orbison, but the instant king was Elvis Presley. From the start, he had it—he was sultry, steamy, loaded, and ready to go, a new kind of country boy who had grown up in a gas station. And he could sing. If you were listening to the "Louisiana Hayride" from Shreveport, Louisiana, in 1954, you would have heard him singing his first hit, "Blue Moon of Kentucky," written, of course, by Bill Monroe.

Caught between the two waves of "uptown" and "rock and roll," country music was in a state of confusion. It was a bad time for artists who couldn't or wouldn't adapt to one trend or the other. Kenny Baker recalls the period:

There was a few years there about the time that this rock and roll came in. It wasn't only bluegrass music, but all of country music shot its wad. Why, they just disbanded left and right down there in Nashville. Of course, Bill kept an outfit, but he damned sure didn't make no money with it. There just wasn't any money to be made in bluegrass or country music then.

It was more than the musical trends of the day that presented problems for someone like Bill. The rural world was changing. Television was bringing a whole new world of entertainment to the people. It provided an escape from their lives into glamorous suburban situation comedies peopled by characters no smarter than they. The whole thrust of television was to bring people into the mainstream of modern, homogenized culture. In order to

71

appeal to the largest audience possible, corners were rounded off, individuality was de-emphasized, highs and lows were eliminated, fantasy was substituted for reality. Naturally, the people loved it. They would stay at home and watch it for hours. Why go out when you could get all the entertainment you needed right in your living room?

Needless to say, television meant the end of live radio, and radio had played

Bill Monroe with his sister *(Photo: Carl Fleischhauer)*

a large part in the spread of Bill's music through the years. Records were the thing now on radio. Disc jockeys were picked for their voices more than for what they knew about music. The audience was primarily teenagers who wanted whatever was the newest, and housewives who wanted a touch of romance in their lives. Elvis Presley and Eddy Arnold did very well. Bill's fans still bought his records steadily and he still recorded frequently, now for the Decca label, but his records weren't often played on the radio. They were "too country." Again, Kenny Baker:

When TV came in all those live radio shows started to run into trouble, and people had the notion that radio didn't mean anything anymore. And that killed business in those small towns.
Before, he used to have an early morning radio show on WSM, and sometimes he'd work the noon farm program and that would all help your local dates and he could afford to pay salaries.

In a sense, everything that Bill represented was being undercut by these various trends. What would happen if he resisted them? How far can a professional entertainer go against the desires of the public and still survive? The question might not have occurred to Bill, or if it did, he might not have thought it relevant. He was a musician above all else, and he had to play his music the way he heard it. He was going to remain true to his culture and his music, and he had faith that his fans would stick with him.

I think that I have the best fans in the world. I've tried my best to take time to treat them right, and they've been the same way with me. They've been my fans right on down through the years. A long time. And they still come to my show, and they want to speak to me every time they come around, and make pictures every year. It's got to where it's a wonderful thing and I enjoy it. It's hard to do. It takes a lot out of you to do all that, but I don't mind. If they're good enough to come to my show, I'm going to go all out to make them welcome.

Despite his faith in what he was doing and his faith in his fans, it wasn't an easy time. Dates weren't coming in the way they used to. It was getting more and more difficult to meet his high overhead. He no longer could carry the ball team with him or any other artists. The summertime was still good, but the winter was thin, and he couldn't keep his men on salary anymore. He could only afford to pay them union scale for each day they played. Jimmy Martin left to form his own group, The Sunny Mountain Boys. He was replaced by another fine singer and guitar player, Ed Mayfield, whose career was cut short by a fatal accident. For the next few years several lead men came and went. The same was true of banjo players. Through much of the time that Jimmy Martin had played with Bill, Rudy Lyle was on banjo. After he left, there were several men who worked with Bill for short periods, but no one who worked steadily for a long time.

Don Reno was one who sensed that things were not right with Bill.

Bill was as particular about his musicians as anybody I have ever seen. If a man couldn't cut it he didn't want him on the stage with him. He tried out guitar picker after guitar picker that today would be class "A," and he would tell him to go home and practice two or three years and come back. I think he lost some of his drive when he got to changing musicians too fast. He was picking men and musicians too—boys that he thought would get in there. But somewhere in the mid-fifties it seems that the caliber of musicians changed. When I was with him money wasn't the object. It was getting something accomplished that you had in you. It was like a fever. The only medicine you could get for it was playing. And Bill had this fever. Somewhere in there he lost it, it seems.

A band has to stay together at least six months before it can play and for a while he would change three or four times in six months and it hurt him. I used to worry about him and if he was in the Roanoke area I would go over with my P.A. system and my guitar just to help him put on a good show. I hate to see a good musician go down. I want to see him stay in there and pitch.

ill and the Bluegrass Boys at a school date *(Photo: Carl Fleischhauer)*

JAMES ROONEY

In spite of the problems of the time and the difficulty in keeping a good group together, Bill continued to get deeper into his music. Now that he wasn't working so many days in the year, he had more time for himself. He spent more time on his farm outside of Nashville, and seemed to welcome the opportunity to get back to the land.

Being on the farm you remember how you growed up. I think it's got its advantage in bluegrass. I really believe it does. If I'd have been a man that drinked and stayed in a beer joint half the time, I can't see that bluegrass would advance. I think it would have went to the dogs. And it would have been that much of my time lost and I wouldn't have known what I was doing or anything.
It has kept me away from a lot of things in Nashville—parties and things— where there might have been some other kind of music coming around that it wouldn't have helped me to have even heard. If I'm on the farm or working around it, why, the music is in the back of my mind or different things or different ideas or different titles or how you think the fiddler would play the best on it—it would be good for him or good for another fiddler—things like that. It hasn't hurt me to have worked on the farm.

A man doesn't always know the way his life is going to go. Bill had always managed to control and shape his life the way he had wanted to. Now, for the first time, he seemed to be at the mercy of trends and events beyond his control. As it was to happen, however, it was not to be all to his disadvantage. Two developments were to affect Bill's career: one, the national folk-song revival; the other, a revival of interest in string-band music in the mid-South, especially in North Carolina and Virginia.
In the mid-fifties in certain cities like New York, Boston, Philadelphia, Chicago, and Berkeley, and at schools like Harvard, Yale, Swarthmore, the University of Chicago, and the University of California at Berkeley, there were groups of people, mostly students, who were becoming interested in American folk music. In New York the interest was fanned and spread by Pete Seeger, Alan Lomax, and the group around Leadbelly and Woody Guthrie. They were all concerned with traditional music as opposed to the

commercial popular music of the day. The movement was given a big boost when the Weavers—which included Pete Seeger, Ronnie Gilbert, Lee Hayes, and Fred Hellerman—broke through the commercial barrier with their recording of Leadbelly's "Irene Goodnight." Everywhere the Weavers went, they would leave behind a group of young people who wanted play folk music. The "folk revival" was on.

At Swarthmore College in Pennsylvania, a group of students decided to devote a weekend to folk music. A student named Ralph Rinzler organized the event, the first of many "folk festivals." After the festival, Ralph was approached by Mike Seeger, Pete's younger half-brother who lived in Washington and was getting interested in bluegrass and old-time music. He suggested to Ralph that he should really include someone like Bill Monroe or the Stanley Brothers on a program of folk music since they were part of a living tradition, not revivalists. Ralph and Mike began to go to outdoor parks where they could hear the music, and a whole new world was opened for Rinzler.

There were a few of us from the city who were following Bill—Mike Seeger, myself, Ray Foshag, Jerry and Alice Foster. Mike and I would go to various parks sorting out who we liked—Bill, the Stanley Brothers, Grampa Jones, Don Reno—but bluegrass had not got into the folk revival. But for me it was like going into another world. I was fascinated by the totally different lifestyle—dinner on the grounds, different speech patterns—a whole different way of life. The whole idea of it really astounded me—that this existed. That was in fifty-four and fifty-five.

Despite the interest of people like Ralph and Mike, Bill's audience was still in the country. As if in reaction to the musical trends in Nashville toward "uptown country" and "rock-a-billy," the people in Virginia, North Carolina, parts of Maryland and Pennsylvania seemed to want more and more bluegrass music. Reno & Smiley, Flatt & Scruggs, Mac Wiseman, the Stanley Brothers, the Osborne Brothers, Bill Clifton, and the Country Gentlemen all worked the area with success. At Union Grove, North Carolina, Galax, Virginia, and several other locations, fiddlers' conventions

Photo: Carl Fleischhauer

were held which drew hundreds of fiddlers, banjo pickers, mandolin pickers, old-time bands, and bluegrass bands. In back of this activity was the man who started it all: Bill Monroe. But it was almost overlooked at times that he had started it. Bill was having trouble keeping a band together for any length of time, and some of the other bands seemed to be able to stay together better and sound better. Ralph Rinzler was keenly aware that things were not as they should be.

The reason Bill was in the dumps in the fifties was the takeover of rock and roll at the time of Elvis Presley, and it threatened all of country music for a while. Another factor was that Flatt and Scruggs had cornered the market on what was left.

Bill was left behind in the way that he was because he stuck hard by what he believed in, and he also had no business organization behind him. Mrs. Scruggs managed their business very shrewdly and the impression was created that bluegrass began and ended with Flatt and Scruggs.

By sixty-one Flatt and Scruggs had come north. Pete Welding wrote an article in *Sing Out!* about how Scruggs had made obsolete everything that had come before it and claimed him as the master of bluegrass music. I was furious and asked to do a story on Monroe.

None of us had ever talked to him. He was very aloof. I asked him if he would give an interview and his reply was, "If you want to know anything about bluegrass, ask Louise Scruggs." And he turned and walked away. Finally however, his companion and bass player for many years, Bessie Lee Mauldin, and Carter Stanley persuaded him.

The one thing he was extremely aware of was that he had fashioned his music. His music didn't happen and it wasn't intuitive. He consciously did it. The way a painter takes his brush and dips his brush into different colors on that palette, he can tell you exactly where he gets every sound in his music.

He has a whole philosophy of why it is important to get something out of a tune that's in it. You get the essence out of a tune by playing the melody. On records he'll play note for note the essence of that tune, but when he gets to the last line he'll play something that's pretty far out and he'll save that, and you'll know that it's coming and he does that so intentionally, and he knows exactly what you're waiting for. All the subtleties in his music are so intentional. He remembers so much from his childhood that he has put into his music. And it's not only a memory. It's a sensitivity to people and values and to beauty.

Once the ways of communication were opened between Ralph and Bill, a relationship was established that meant a great deal to both of them. Ralph was heavily involved in the folk revival both as a member of a group called the Greenbriar Boys and as a director of the Newport Folk Festival. In 1963 he decided to strengthen their relationship by moving to Nashville where he handled Bill's booking, especially in the non-country market. Working closely with Bill gave Ralph a deeper understanding of him as a man.

Some of the things that really struck me about Bill came out of a trip that he and Del McCoury and I took to Rosine. We got in a truck and drove from Nashville with a pig and a couple of hound dogs. He gave the pig to his brother Speed and the hounds to Charlie. And that night Bill and Charlie and Del and I went out all of us to the woods and listened to those dogs bay and Bill could tell which one was which. And the next day we went and Bill showed me his parents' grave and said, "That was a true song, just like I told you." On the stones it says "Gone but not forgotten" and "We'll meet again someday" exactly as it is in the song. And then Bill walked back up the hill from town toward his parents' house which is on a disused road and explained, "When I was a boy this was a wagon path. This was the main road into Rosine, and everyone who wanted to get to Rosine went past our house and would stop. I came up that hill after I had been away from home and it was the first time I had seen the house dark and I wrote that song 'I'm On My Way Back to the Old Home.' " And you can see how many of his songs tell his life story. It's the reason there is so much passion in his mandolin break in that song.

He said, "You know, people used to come to this house and since I was cross-eyed strangers would laugh at me and I couldn't see well enough to

play ball. After a while when I saw strangers coming down that road I would go and hide in the barn because I didn't want them to laugh at me." So he was a real outcast.
And then we walked into the barn and the floor was strewn with letters and papers—his father's ledgers. And he was just like Bill; he wrote down everything. He picked up everything and put it in the trunk and explained that he really was at a loss to understand how his brothers could strew things that belonged to his father around like that. He had a deep respect for his parents and a great feeling for them as links with the past.

Another man who had given some thought to Bill's situation was a country music promoter. Carlton Haney put together a program at Berryville, Virginia, of the most popular bluegrass bands in the area with Bill headlining as a special attraction. All of the bands performed separately. When Bill came out with Don Reno and Mac Wiseman to recreate some of their songs from ten years ago, the effect was electric. Bill seemed to come to life as he responded to the shouts of the crowd for the various numbers, and it soon became clear to the crowd who was the boss of the stage. It was the seed of an idea for Carlton. Why not put on a bluegrass festival with Bill as its focus, acknowledging him as the master of the music he had created? It was to take Carlton a few years to bring the idea to fruition, but it was to prove to be a vital element in Bill's comeback.
Another important element was to be a significant improvement in personnel, the source of which was a surprise. Up in Cambridge a young banjo player named Bill Keith and I had formed a bluegrass band. Bill was one of Pete Seeger's sprouts, having learned to play five-string banjo from Pete's instruction book. He had then set out to master Earl Scrugg's style of playing the banjo and was beginning to develop his own style that would enable him to play a fiddle tune such as "The Devil's Dream" note for note. No banjo player had ever done this before, and Keith's reputation was starting to spread. In the fall of sixty-two he decided to try his wings with a full-time band, and he joined Red Allen and his Kentuckians in Washington, D.C. At this time he met Earl Scruggs, who asked him to visit him in Nashville to talk about an instruction book that Earl was working on. While there, Earl took Keith down

to the Opry and he was jamming backstage. Monroe came in, listened for a while, and went out. Later, he sent word via Kenny Baker that if Keith wanted a job he could have it. It was a month before Keith joined Bill, and when he did it was the start of an extremely productive relationship.

When I joined Bill it was pretty intense. I got there on Thursday, officially tried out on Friday night, joined the union Saturday, and played on the Opry Saturday night. And then we recorded right away, which I regretted because the music improved greatly as the band stayed together.
Bill's music had a lot of effect on me. Strangely enough, I hadn't heard a lot of his music before I went to work for him. I'd listened a lot to banjo things—Scruggs and Reno—and his earlier things—but I didn't know any words—so everything he did had a big effect on me. I remember picking up dynamic ideas he would use where he would play the first lines of a break in one style and then change styles in the last line. I remarked on that. I remembered the variations he would go through, playing one song week in and week out. A lot of things would happen and I would notice them. So hearing his playing had quite an effect on me. One thing—it made me use the style that I had put together less and less in standard bluegrass material and limit it to instrumentals and fiddle tunes and breaks.
He hadn't played some fiddle tunes I played very much before I joined up. He hadn't done "The Sailor's Hornpipe," but he did learn the tune. We recorded it without a mandolin break, but before too long he was playing it, and I took it as an indication that he wanted to play that style.
He never told me how to play something. I could sometimes tell by the way he played and reacted how he felt about something. When I went to work for him I said, "I really don't know what the rules are, and if I do something outrageous, don't hesitate to tell me about it." He never did say anything. Although one time we were playing "Footprints in the Snow" and I put in part of "Nola" and he got back up to the mike and sang the last verse, leaving out about three or four verses and that's how I knew what his reaction was. It wasn't a very comfortable situation. It wasn't my prerogative to do that to his tune.
My style didn't change much. It was my technique. When I went there I had

mastered most of the rolls. I had my vocabulary; I just improved my technique—phrasing, timing. Earl, on the other hand, when he first was with Bill used mostly a forward roll, but he added considerably to his vocabulary while he was with Bill and really defined his style.
I improved a lot with Bill. You couldn't help it. You wanted to. It felt great. It was always getting better. It was a tonic.
Each man in the band has something completely different from what anyone else onstage has, and you're doing just what you want to on it. And it's a great feeling.

For Monroe, having Keith with him was a tonic, too. "Brad" (there was only one Bill in the band, so William Bradford Keith became "Brad") gave him what he needed—a challenge—and his music found its drive again.

Brad Keith, he understands music. He's a good listener and he's a good man to listen to. He's done a lot of good for music and especially for bluegrass. At a time when I needed a boost, I think that Brad gave it to me. I think it just came in when I needed it. Before he came along no banjo player could play those old fiddle numbers right. You have to play like Brad could play or you would be faking your way through a number. It's learned a lot of banjo players what to do and how to do it to where they can come along and fill that bill today.

As time strengthened their friendship, both Bill and Brad realized that there was more to the other than just music. As Keith tells it:

The more I got to know him, the more important he as a musical figure seemed to be, but I also could see there was more to him than music, and that's what you get to know.
We started out with a very unstructured personal relationship. After a couple of months, things seemed to be looser, more down home. And even since those

days he has mellowed a lot. One day up at Bill's park in Beanblossom someone came back to meet Bill and Bill was busy and kind of short with him. The guy didn't have anything to say, he just came back to look and poke and so he struck up a conversation and Bill had nothing to say. He had things to do, so the fellow stood there for a minute, and he said, "You know, you ain't as

left to right: Bessie Lee Mauldin, Billy Baker, Bill Keith, Bill Monroe, and Del McCoury *(Photo: David Gahr)*

jolly as you used to be." And Bill just broke up. He thought that was very funny. He would repeat that line for months.

He's said that for him the most rewarding day would be to get up very early and have a big breakfast, go out and work in the fields all morning, take about a one-hour nap at lunch and get back out and work till dusk and relax and take a bath and then get onstage somewhere and play some music and then get in the car and drive. That's his formula and he spent a lot of Saturdays like that.

In turn, Monroe says,

When Brad was with me he was digging deep in bluegrass. He learned what I dug deep and the sound that I would search for and what I would set aside and keep. It means so much to have a good friend in bluegrass later on in life. You don't know how good it really makes you feel. In the early days with life ahead of me and everything, why, I figured I didn't need any help, because I could work hard.

I take more pains with my music now than I did when I was young. When you're young you go through a lot of music and you don't take enough time to really get into it. In the early days I was really fast with a mandolin and I played the notes clean. But today it seems that I can put more into it.

Brad Keith wanted to help it and put his heart in bluegrass music, and there's other people that have helped it.

Ralph Rinzler noticed the change in Bill. It wasn't an overnight thing. There were times when Bill would be totally removed from those around him, unhappy with something that had happened, but gradually he was opening up and responding to the stimulus from outside his "world."

Sometimes after not talking for days in the car he'd wake up at three o'clock in the morning and you could be driving the car and he'd start talking to you about anything for five hours without stopping. And you could ask him any

question and he would tell you exactly what was on his mind.

Having Bill Keith come with him reinforced his musical vitality. Keith would hear one of Monroe's phrases and he could pick it up and instantly he would echo it back on the banjo and that would excite Monroe because it was an acknowledgment of the subtlety of his creativity right there on the stage.

It also showed Monroe that his music was universal enough that a college-educated fellow from a well-to-do family would think enough of his music to be able to play it that way and then come to Nashville and work with him.

The thing about his relationship to the revival was that once he started to talk to Keith, play with Keith, and play at city functions where people understood him with their minds as well as their souls, he realized how much people thought about his music in the way that he did. But I think that before he hit the folk revival audience he had never discussed his music intellectually the way he does now.

And the kids coming to his music discovered that he maintained an incredibly high standard for his music and had a deep philosophy about how music can and should be played.

If anything has made him mellow as a person it is the realization that he is accepted as a thinker and a spokesman for his music verbally as well as musically.

After Keith left the band, others began to come into it from the "outside" world. There was Steve Arkin and Gene Lowinger from New York, who served brief hitches on banjo and fiddle; Pete Rowan, a fine lead singer and guitar player from Cambridge; Richard Greene, a virtuoso fiddler from California; Lamar Greer, a thoughtful banjo player from Washington; Roland White, a lead singer from Maine via California; Byron Berline, a champion fiddler from Oklahoma; and Vic Jordan, another fine banjo picker from Washington.

The pattern changed in another respect. When these "boys" left Bill, it wasn't necessarily to play in another bluegrass band or to form one of their own in the manner of Flatt, Scruggs, Reno, or Martin. They went out into music. Bill Keith explains his feelings about it:

Keith *(Photo: Carl Fleischhauer)*

BOSSMAN BILL MONROE

Since I left Bill I've gone through some musical changes. I didn't feel that the thing for me to do then was to organize another bluegrass band, even if I did new material.
By the time I left the band was very tight, and after playing in that kind of situation it seemed very anticlimatic to play in a bluegrass situation—to get a fiddle, mandolin—everything in concert. It just didn't seem right. I just went on a trip to England to just play music. It was the thing to do. When I got back I could have gone back but I didn't give it a thought. It just didn't seem to be the thing to do. But bluegrass is a great way to get into music, and you can see how many musicians have been through Bill's band. He has maintained his sound just as if there was no turnover with no charts or written music.

Keith went on to play in the Jim Kweskin Jug Band, then he played pedal steel guitar with Ian & Sylvia, and currently is with Geoff & Maria Muldaur. Pete Rowan formed a group called Earth Opera and then joined Richard Greene in a group called Sea Train. Byron Berline has worked with the Dillard and Clark Expedition and has recorded with the Rolling Stones. This development wasn't lost on Bill. He came to regard bluegrass as a training ground for musicians, not just bluegrass musicians. They became extensions of himself wherever they went. He remained a part of them.

Now recently a lot of fine young musicians have been with me—Brad Keith, Pete Rowan, Richard Greene, Steve Arkin, Gene Lowinger, Byron Berline. They got to loving this music, you know. It's a good music to learn on. I think when you can play bluegrass, you can really play any kind of music, if you really wanted to. You could go right from bluegrass into jazz or anything. You know, it got into Pete's blood to be a bluegrass guitar man and singer. And of course Brad, I guess, I don't know where he started learning, but it was a good push to banjo playing. And Richard made into a good fiddler. I

to: David Gahr

Photo: David Gahr

guess he loves the fiddle as well as anybody in the world. But you know Richard got that jazz in his mind, that he was going to be a great bandleader of nothing but jazz, and that proves how hard it gets after you get out on your own. It takes backing to get that stuff going. Arkin could play the best back-up banjo I have ever heard. He could beat Brad all over playing a back-up. Now there ain't no way around it. He could do it. He could put stuff in it and make it sell. Brad might put the same kind of stuff in it but it wouldn't do what that boy could do with it. But he couldn't carry a melody like Brad could do it.

Now he's got a number of mine and Pete Rowan's got a number of mine. The one that Pete's got is a song that I made when he was in Montreal the first trip and Arkin's got a good banjo number. But it had to come from him before we could get it straightened out. And Pete's got this other number that had to come out of him to get it. That's a fine number, man. It's got a lot of music in it. Deeper than bluegrass needs to play. It would take a good band to play it. But that's two numbers that I need to get ahold of, because they belong to me.

Bill could now see that the message of his music had gotten through, that he was not alone in finding significance in it. He could see himself as an important link between the past and the future. He conceived of instrumentals that would capture his feelings about times past.

"Crossing The Cumberlands." We had broken down in our bus up there on the Cumberland mountains and while I was sitting there I could picture the pioneers heading West and how slow they was going and what kind of trouble they was having. It was a hard go—a lot of rough days and nights— and that was my kind of a sound that I thought would fit in with the way they was having to travel and the hard times they was having and the way they was feeling. "Crossing The Cumberlands" has sort of a mournful touch to it— kind of Indian tones to it—written in A minor. That could have been the way it was one day and the next day the sun could have been shining after camping

Paul Butterfield and Mike Bloomfield *(Photo: David Ga*

92

the night and they would have felt like moving on. That's my way of looking at life and music and the way people would have felt years ago. I don't know how other people would think about things like that.

"Land of Lincoln." I was trying to picture the way I figured things would be back in Abraham Lincoln's day, when he was a young man and practicing law or something like that and, say, he could hear this old fiddler and he could be playing a number that would sound like this one so I called it "The Land of Lincoln." I believe that that's about as far back as anybody will ever go and pick up tunes for a fiddle number. I might study up more tunes later on, but that goes back a long way. And the song has got a meaning to it for the man that's a-playing it or people that would listen to it—but especially for the man that's playing it. It's doing something for him. It's a lonesome type of number, if you notice. He could be telling a story. And I could picture Lincoln as he would pass this old fiddler. Maybe he would be sitting out someplace playing—along the road or on a streetcorner or something and, playing the fiddle, and, say, he would stop and listen to that number, you know. I could picture something like that. Abraham Lincoln was a railsplitter and he was bound to like old-time fiddling. And that makes you know that he would like that kind of a tune. I just can't keep from believing that he could.

I know my Uncle Pen Vanderver would've liked that kind of a tune.

To refresh the fundamental strength of his music, Bill is now returning to the fiddle numbers he learned from his Uncle Pen forty years ago. He has remembered them note for note and carried them in his head through the years. He mentioned them to Kenny Baker the first time Baker was with Bill.

After I got to playing his stuff a little bit, he told me about these old numbers of his Uncle Pen's. He said he was saving them back for the right fiddler, the man he thought could play them and do them right. That's what he told me the first time I worked for him. They've got that old sound and that drive is in there. I've listened to fiddle music all my life and some of those numbers I've never heard before. Had he been a fiddler, boy, he would've been something else.

BOSSMAN BILL MONROE

To be recording these numbers now after so many years is giving Bill a good deal of pleasure and satisfaction. He is proud to be able to hand them on to another generation of musicians. His musical memory is flawless.

I don't know how I have remembered all of Uncle Pen's tunes. It's a mystery. 'Cause it's been a long time. I would touch them up maybe once or twice a year. But there was a lot of years in the early part of bluegrass music that I

Photo: Carl Fleischhauer

was so busy that I didn't fool with them much. Uncle Pen passed away when I was eighteen or nineteen years old, I guess. And that's been a long time ago. And to remember them numbers! I don't think there's been many got away from me. There might have been one or two that slipped my mind—but numbers like "Jenny Lynn," "White Folks Ain't Treatin' Me Right," "Methodist Preacher," "Candy Gal," "Goin' Up Caney," numbers like that, stayed right with me all through the years.

Playing these numbers has reinforced Bill's deepest feelings about the way music should be played, and he wants to make sure that others get the message.

I have followed instrumental numbers for so long that I know how they should go. I know if it is getting out of line. I know the minute if you leave the melody and go on someone else's tune. That's studying it and listening to tones and knowing what tone should follow another. Now I know that tunes like "Roanoke" or "Turkey in the Straw" don't need changing. They've got everything in them they need. Now if you could come up and play the same melody in another position, why I'm 100 percent for it. So if you've heard a fiddler all your life—maybe you've danced after him—he still hasn't put enough time on it to really learn how it should be played—maybe he was playing for a square dance and making money and that's all he was interested in. He wasn't interested to learn the number and play it the right way. And that's when a man should learn to follow the melody is when he's a young boy. He should take time to learn which way it should go and go that way. If it's "Fire on the Mountain" or any number like that that's got the notes the way the man wrote it and if it sounds good to you and you think he did a good job with it, you should put every note in it that he did if you can. You shouldn't leave anything out. Many banjo players will cut through and hide behind their licks and not take time to learn which way the melody goes and what notes should follow the other.

If you've played music all your life, when you get on up in years you see the

Bill Monroe and Mac Wiseman *(Photo: David G*

BOSSMAN BILL MONROE

things that you've done for people and you want to do more for them as you get older. I guess there's many times when I could have been helped too in the way of a mandolin but if you're running something—if you're the boss of it, why, there's not everybody coming along and saying, "Well, you play it this way. You're not playing it right." They think, "If I said that, he might fire me." I guess everybody could be helped at times.

Bill Monroe,
Tex Logan
and Don Reno
(Photo: David Gahr)

Although Bill doesn't play as many dates today as he did twenty years ago, the range of his audiences is wider than ever. There are concerts at places like Carnegie Hall in New York, Jordan Hall in Boston; at the big folk festivals like Newport, Philadelphia, or Mariposa; at schools like Harvard, the University of Chicago, or the University of California at Berkeley; at blue-grass clubs which have been formed in Toronto, Montreal, Cambridge, and

JAMES ROONEY

Photo: David Gahr

BOSSMAN BILL MONROE

New York; at outdoor parks from Pennsylvania to Louisiana; at country music clubs in the mid-Northern cities; on country music package shows in big arenas; at county and state fairs; and at an increasing number of bluegrass festivals based on Carlton Haney's idea of many bands with Bill as the central figure. The most important of these is now at Bill's own park, the Brown County Jamboree in Beanblossom, Indiana, near Bloomington.
The Beanblossom Festival is a living summation of Bill's career. People come from all over the United States and Canada—college students, bluegrass musicians, rock musicians, country musicians, folklorists, farmers, truck drivers, mechanics, housewives—everyone who has been touched by Bill's music. The concerts go on for three days and feature as many musicians who have played with Bill through the years as can make it: Clyde Moody, Jim Eanes, Mac Wiseman, Jimmy Martin, Del McCoury, Earl Scruggs, Don Reno, Sonny Osborne, Rudy Lyle, Bill Keith, Chubby Wise, Howdy Forrester, Benny Martin, Vassar Clements, Bobby Hicks, Tex Logan. Of course, Bill's current band is featured as well which includes his son, James Monroe, singing lead, Rual Yarborough on banjo, and Kenny Baker on fiddle. There are fiddle workshops, banjo workshops, a sacred concert Sunday morning, and a concert featuring the highlights of Bill's career.
In his music Bill Monroe has summed up the essence of the culture he inherited. He refined it and passed it back to his own people and out to the world at large. This is what has given Bill Monroe's music and life meaning and significance.
In his office in Nashville, Bill has the usual plaques and awards that an artist receives as symbols of a rewarding career. But what catches the eye is a painting of an old man, weatherbeaten, with long white hair, a white moustache, and deeply sunk eyes. Around his head float pieces of written music.

That really works like an old-timer though, don't it? Look at that nose— crooked just a little bit. I've seen a lot of people that had a nose like that. And his eyes are set back in there, boy. And the wrinkles across his forehead. He looks like he's really sure of what he's done, gonna do—with that sheet music up there tore just a little bit—he's looking now further on in life. He's looking just a little past that music.

101

BOSSMAN: MUDDY WATERS

Get out a map. Look at the state of Mississippi. Let your eye travel up the serpentine coils of the Mississippi River until you see the city of Clarksdale. Just a little bit north and west of Clarksdale is the town of Stovall. You're right in the black earth shadow of the river now, in the heart of Coahoma County, about seventy-five miles southwest of Memphis off of Route 61. Stovall isn't a town really. It's a plantation. Thirty years ago, you might have found there a little group playing music for a dance or a party on the plantation. They were all older men except for one strong, young singer. His name was McKinley Morganfield, but they called him Muddy.

Alan Lomax discovered me. He was a young man then. He came through. Really what he was looking for was Robert Johnson but Robert had got killed. And somebody pointed me out to him and he come out and found me. And he recorded me right in my house with my little group. It had a mandolin and a violin. That was a hot group. I was the youngest one in the thing but I could sing, you know. I was in my teens, see, and they was all older men but he was a good mandolin player and also the violin player was good. Yeah—ha, ha—they used to take me round get to the dances and things. You know they'd take me around with 'em 'cause I've always been a vocal. I was stroking a guitar too, a little old wooden guitar. Yeah—think I had a little old Stella, good little old guitar. I made it do what I wanted to do with it, you know. I had that thing. They taken me around 'cause from a young kid up I could sing, you know. We had a lot of little dance things we'd do, you know, but then we'd get down and play those flatfoot blues and that's when I'd come in with my singing, you know. I made up a lot of songs myself just out of the blue sky, you know, a whole lot of songs—then I'd pinch off of some other songs I heard and all that. But most of the time I'd just make 'em dry out of the blue sky all by myself, 'cause I could think then, 'fore I got older.

The recordings that were made that day were the first glimpse the outside world had of Muddy Waters's talent, and that glimpse was only available to scholars. But even before this Muddy had determined that he would have to escape from the world he had been born into. It had barely progressed from pre-Civil War days.

I was picking cotton, pulling corn, milking cows—ha, ha, ha, driving tractors, doing all that stuff; yeah, I've been a farmer. There wasn't too much happening in the thirties in the country—there wasn't nothing happening if you want to know something—but I was there, that's the way I lived—but how I don't know. I worked for 50 cents a day, you know, and 75 cents a day. My brothers and sisters wasn't raised with me, you see. My uncle was raising me. There was two of us. I was raised with my grandmother. That made me and my uncle be raised together. There was two of us. My brothers and sisters, they was raised with their father. They was doing the same thing when they was old enough. Working for that little old 75 cents a day. If it don't rain you make three dollar, seventy-five cent a week. If it don't rain, you know. You could buy groceries at that time with three dollars. You could buy three dollars of groceries and you could get a lot of groceries. Today you buy one item, two items—it costs you five dollars. That's one thing that was different. I don't know how we survived myself, but we made it. We went through some—I paid my dues, I'll tell you that.

It didn't take Muddy long to realize that the music that always seemed to be in him could become the means of making his escape.

I used to beat on a five-gallon can when I was a kid, kerosene you know, used to beat on the bottom of it and sing. "I don't want no woman to chollyham my bone." I'd beat on that can and sing that all day long. I still don't know what that means. There's a old fella give me a old piece of squeeze box. I never did do nothing with it. It was old. I sort of ramshacked it on out you know. Then I picked up a thing they call a jew's harp. I started to beating

it. I got it to go some. Then I switched over to the harmonica—french harp, we called it. Anyway, I got on the harmonica. I got that to go big for me. My grandmother told me when I first picked that harmonica up, she said, "Son, you're sinning. You're playing for the devil. Devil's gonna get you." So, I was playing with a boy named Scott Brown. We was playing together. I was blowing the harp. He'd played guitar. I kept watching. Him and other fellas. First guitar I got cost me two dollars and fifty cents. I saved nickels and dimes until I got two dollars and fifty cents, and I bought it from a young man named Ed Moore. He sold it to me for two dollars and fifty cents and the first time I played on it I made fifty cents at one of those all-night places. And then the man who run it raised me to two-fifty a night, and I knew I was doing right. Then I got one from Sears Roebuck that cost eleven dollars. I had a beautiful box then.

I went to St. Louis to see what I could do, but I couldn't get nothing there. It's hard, you know, if you don't have any friends or family to help you. So I went straight back to Clarksdale. And I got slick then. I had seen people playing on the street corners collecting nickels and dimes and I said, "I know I can do that. I'm gonna do that myself." So I went back on the corner of Fourth Street and it was a wonderful thing. I had my cigar box sitting out there, and I was sitting up on a Coca-Cola box, and I had such a crowd that the police moved me. So I went over to Sunflower, and every time they run me from one corner I'd go to another one. So by closing time—about twelve o'clock at night—I'd have twenty or thirty dollars. One time I made forty dollars and said, "I ain't gonna play no more. This is it."

From the start Muddy had a drive to be the best. And in order to be the best you had to learn from the best. He began to study the styles of the acknowledged masters in the area. The king was Robert Johnson. He had recorded and traveled throughout the area, and his guitar playing set the standard for all bluesmen in the Delta region. But he was killed when Muddy was a young man, and his crown passed to Son House, who today, in his seventies, can still make men weep with the intensity of his playing.

I really admired music so much—but if they was singing good blues, I just

loved 'em. But my copy was Son House. He traveled through the area and lived on a plantation too—one way across from me. He didn't never be still like me, 'cause he'd do a lot of traveling all over the Delta. And any time I could get a chance to hear him play, I'd go. And there was some more good boys down around there with the bottlenecks that's never been known, never been heard of. James Smith. Never been heard of—and really they could do about as much with a bottleneck as Son House or me or anybody else. And that's a shame, you know. They've never been heard of. Never been known. And they could take care of that slide guitar good as me, or anybody I ever heard. That was the Delta sound. That slide guitar. I don't know how it began. It looks easy. It might be easier than picking, but to be a master you've got to know what you're doing there. You've got to know blues to go down in and get some of it and get out of it, you know. I had it in my mind even then to either play music or preach or do something that I would be known, that people would know me. I kept that on my mind. I wanted to be a known person. All of my life. That's what I worked for. I wanted to be internationally known. And I worked on it, from when I was a kid up.

I used to belong to church. I was a good old Baptist, singing in church. A hard shell Baptist (ha, ha). I guess most of that is kind of based upon the same thing. So I got all of my good moaning and trembling going on for me right out of church. Used to be in church every Sunday. I had this mind. I wanted to be one of these things. I wanted to be known. I wanted to be an outstanding man. I wanted to be known by some peoples. Not just two or three peoples knowing me. I wanted to be known around the country. So whatever I was gonna do I was gonna do it good. I think I would've made a good preacher. I believe I would have made a good preacher.

It was all there in him when he made those first recordings. He would play along with the older men, getting with the guitar to keep time behind the mandolin and violin on the dance tunes. He was having a good time. He liked

ddy Waters, Son House *(Photo: David Gahr)*

playing with others. There was more going on and it was more fun than being a solo. It was a feeling that would stay with him.

Playing with that group at Stovall really gave me a feeling for being in a band. Before that it had just been a harmonica and me or the mandolin and me. But you've got a lot of empty spaces. But when you've got four, five, or six pieces working you've always got a full bed of music there for you, waiting on you.

Something else that would be in him from these early years was a feeling that his music meant something to God and the world. It would be his way of living and helping himself and helping others.

> *Why don't you live so God can use you, anywhere, anytime?*
> *Why don't you sing so God can use you, anywhere, anytime?*
> *Why don't you walk so God can use you, anywhere, anytime?*
> *Why don't you moan so God can use you, anywhere, anytime?*

But most of all, he had mastered the blues he had learned from Robert Johnson and Son House. He would sing Johnson's "Walkin' Blues" or his own copy, "The Country Blues," and you could tell he was on top of the singing, a young man, no longer a boy. There was a bite in his diction, a power in his voice, a resonance that came from his chest and powerful frame. And every phrase he sang would be answered by his guitar, trembling, crying, singing, with him. He had learned from the masters and had made it his own.

> *If I'm feelin' tomorrow like I feel today,*
> *I'm gonna pack my suitcase and make my getaway.*
> *Lord I'm troubled, have a worried mind,*
> *And I've never been satisfied,*
> *And I just can't keep from cryin'.*

It was time to go. St. Louis hadn't worked out, but there was still Chicago.
It was a long way, but he knew he at least had some family and friends there,
so he decided to take a chance and make the break. He was twenty-eight,
strong, with nothing to lose, and with a stand up and take it approach
to life.

**Coming up though this life you've got to have some hassles. You just don't
walk in and say, "Here I am. Take me."
I came up to Chicago on a train. Alone. With a suitcase, one suit of clothes,
and a guitar.
Few weeks, couple of weeks or so, I was living on the South Side, 3656
Calumet, about a block west of King's Drive—with some school kids. We'd
grown up together. Then in a couple of weeks I found my peoples here on the
West Side. I had a bunch of cousins then—and I moved over there. Before six
months time I had my own four-room apartment. Ha, ha, ha. That's luck,
man. My own four-room apartment. People was paying high price for rent.
This place I was paying twelve dollars a month—had to furnish my own heat,
pay for my own gas and everything—twelve dollars a month. My cousin that
was living right next to me, he was paying thirty-five dollars a month. Had to
do the same thing, furnish his own gas and everything.
Got a job right away. Got here Saturday morning, got a job Saturday
evening. Boy, luck was with me. Working in a paper factory. Containers.
Swing shift three to eleven in the evening. And I thought I had a good job.
Paper—man, that's some of the heaviest jive you ever seen in your life.**

Muddy may have come to Chicago alone, but thousands came with him.
Thousands were escaping from the back- and mind-breaking economy of the
rural South to get work in the factories of the North. Without money, a place
to live, or a job they came, getting off the train every day to walk into Chicago
ready to take their chances. Like Muddy they would find a friend or relative
from "back home" who would put them up until they got straightened out.
But they would still stick together, alone in a strange Northern city. They
would stay together in the three- and four-family houses and the tenements
of the South Side, far from the big buildings and dynamism of the down-

town area. Those who could get work, worked hard, and on Saturday night they would get together and think about "home"—Mississippi, the Delta, the slow life on the land that seemed so far away. And they would hire a little music to help ease their Chicago troubles, help them get "back home," help them stay alive in Chicago.

Then I started playing around Saturday nights at parties at peoples' houses. Just myself.

From the house parties, the next step was to work in the countless little clubs and lounges that were springing up on street corners in every neighborhood. They weren't fancy and could occasionally get a little rough, but it was where the people and the money were. Muddy Waters was not slow or unsure about finding the right pathway to achieve his aim of becoming a "known person." He was going out and getting it for himself.

And then the little clubs began to find out about me then. Then I got with a boy named Blue Smitty. Then Jimmy Rodgers. I was working five days a week and playing six, seven nights a week. My little five dollars a night to play, you know. In music then you'd go in and tell the people you played blues; a lot of 'em they'd shake their head and say, "Sorry, can't use you."
First money I made in a club was fifty-two dollars a week after the little five dollars a night. Six nights a week. I was at the Flame, on Indiana, between Thirtieth and Thirty-first. I went in with little Eddie Boyd, playing sideman for him. He was here when I got here. Played sideman for him, sideman for Sunnyland Slim, couple of times with Memphis Slim. Memphis Slim was the big man, he was the big man. I didn't get a chance to sing very much. I was just playing the guitar. I played with Sonny Boy too, you know—not Rice Miller. Something funny. I played with Sonny Boy one night. We was out there. He got high. You know he was kind of a lush a little, and oh, he got to where he couldn't sing and asked me if I could sing one. And I sung my song and I brought the housetop down. Ha, ha. He got so mad. It was

"Troubles All In The World I See," and I brought the housetop completely down. And Sonny Boy—he's dead now, I wouldn't lie on him—and he got so sore and went to singing himself.

Jimmy Rogers

Muddy had more in his head than money and "becoming known." He was thinking about his music. At the house parties he had sung by himself and had played acoustic guitar. It was the same as it had been back home, but in the clubs it was different.

111

When I went into the clubs, the first thing I wanted was an amplifier.
Couldn't nobody hear you with an acoustic. Wherever you've got booze
you're going to get a little fight. You get a more pure thing out of an acoustic,
but you get more noise out of an amplifier. The first amplified guitar I can
remember hearing was over in Helena, Arkansas, over KFFA. I went across
the river with Sonny Boy Williamson—Rice Miller. He had a radio program
there and there was a boy playing an electric guitar—Joe Willie Wilcomb. So
every week I would go over there and they would let me sit in with them on
the program. So that's what I got when I went into the clubs.

Beyond the amplified sound of the guitar which could cut through the
talking, hustling, laughing, and fighting in those clubs, Muddy was getting
into his music and meeting men who could get into it with him.

If I hadn't come up here I really don't know what would have happened. I
did Chicago a lot of good. A lot of people here didn't hear Son or Robert
Johnson 'cause they didn't get a chance to. But all by itself that sound never
would have made it in Chicago. I guess I'm just one of the first people who
was thinking of that sound and kept it in my mind, learning on that sound,
and when I got here I found peoples that could get close to that sound. One
thing I knew I wanted was that harp sound. I guess I loved the harp 'cause
that's the first thing I learned on. Always liked the harp sound.
First harpman I ever heard was Johnny Brown in Mississippi. Just plain old
harp—no amplifier. He was really up to date with it. He was a blowing man.
He could blow.
When I came to Chicago Jimmy Rodgers was my first harp blower, then he
went to guitar. He's a Mississippi boy and he had the bluesy sound and he
combined it with that sound of mine and it fit it.
When I run up on Little Walter he just fitted me. He's from Alexandria,
Louisiana, up from Shreveport. Little Walter, he was a good little hustler.
He'd play with you or get him a gig by himself, get him a guitar player and
go on and do it. I played a gig with him one night. Sideman. Before I got
going. Yeah, I played a couple of gigs with him.

He had a thing on the harp that nobody had. And today they're still trying for it, but they can't come up to it. It really fitted in with me, what I was doing and—he was much younger than me, but he could really understand the

Little Walter

blues and he knew what to put in there and when to put it in there. So all I can say is that he is the greatest I've ever heard.

It was no accident that Walter and Jimmy were from that Delta country too. A hundred miles east or west and you were into a different sound, and Muddy could tell the difference.

But Baby Face Leroy on guitar never did fit very good. He was from Mobile, Alabama. It seems funny, but Texas is a different sound from Mississippi. Mississippi and Louisiana are close together, then over in Alabama and Georgia it's a whole lot different. It seems funny, but that's the way it is. Well, that Delta sound is the one that I brought to Chicago. There was a lot was in that groove in Mississippi but they didn't get the chance to bring it out. I knowed a lot of 'em could play as good as Robert, but didn't get the chance to bring it up North so they could expose it out to the public. It's too bad, too. I had it in my mind I wanted to do this particular thing. I wanted to play close 'round Son House, between Son and Robert, and I got in there with it. My particular style is based on their style, but is not exactly like them. I wanted to play between those two. I know Robert could beat me sliding (ha, ha, ha). I guess "old man" (Son House)—he's done got old now, but when he was young I guess he could beat me sliding. I guess both could. Maybe, I don't know. But they wasn't doing too much with the singing part, 'specially the old man. I don't think either one of 'em could really do too much with me singing—even Robert. Robert had a sweet voice, but it was kind of a high-pitched voice, you know. I got a lower-pitched voice.

Listen to that voice as the man sings. Rocking his body just enough to get with the beat, barking out the words:

> *Well I'm going away to leave, won't be back no more*
> *Goin' back down South, child, don't you want to go?*
> *Lord I'm troubled, I be all worried mind.*

Photo: David C

JAMES ROONEY

Babe, I just can't be satisfied
And I just can't keep from cryin.' *

Listen to him moan:

Well I woke
Up this mornin' feelin' 'round
 'round for my shoes,
You can tell by that, man, I've got them old
 them old walkin' blues.
Woke up this morning,
Feelin' 'round, feelin' 'round, for my shoes
Well you can
Tell by that child
Hey
I've got the walkin' blues. †

The words take on a life of their own as Muddy's voice goes over them, twisting them, shaping them, making them tremble with his guitar, making them wince with his face as he gets them out, using them to cast a spell as they dissolve at the end of the verse. Then his eyes open wide and that barrel chested voice booms out with the start of the next verse or the next song and gives you what you want—authority. He is singing the blues with a weight and force and subtlety (there is no getting down on his knees) that no one else has. He brings his little band along with him, riding over the waves of people in the little room. He is talking to them about who he is, about his troubles and a woman and being from the country in the big city. And that's what they want to hear—what they need to hear. But he sings in such a way that he is

---

* "I Can't Be Satisfied" *by Muddy Waters* ©1959 *Arc Music Corp. Used with permission of the publisher; all rights reserved.*

† "Walkin' Blues" *by Willie Dixon* ©1966 *Arc Music Corp. Used with permission of the publisher; all rights reserved.*

always standing, always in charge, never put down, never whining or apologizing for being who he is. Muddy Waters was finally where he belonged —in front of a band.

We put Leroy on drums, Jimmy Rodgers on guitar, I had guitar, and Little Walter on harp. It was my band. My band. Period. And then we stayed like that for a few years.

Within two years of coming to Chicago, Muddy had established himself. He had found the right men to play his music, and his audience was starting to find him in ever-increasing numbers. But it's one thing to be a good singer in one out of a hundred clubs, and another to be a "star" and be "known." As soon as Muddy left the club and went back to his apartment he was just another person—the guy who lives upstairs. He wanted more than that, and he knew that the only way to get what he wanted was to make a record.

To get a name, you got to get a record. People lived right up under me, they didn't know who I was until I got a record out. Then they say, "He live right there!"—got to get a record. I got a hit thing the first one I got. I call's it luck. It was a big blues seller amongst the black peoples. Chess had a talent scout. He looked me up. Sunnyland told him about me and all that—Sunnyland Slim—told him about how good I could sing. They come looking for me. So when I first made the record, Leonard Chess, he had a girl with him, I think her name was Evelyn then—that was his partner—and he couldn't understand —he didn't dig what I did. He held me up about a year. So we did it in forty-six—must have been long about the fall of the year—and it came out in forty-seven in March or April. Recorded four. Recorded "Feel Like Goin' Home," "Can't Be Satisfied," and "Little Annie Mae" and "Gypsy Woman." All my stuff.

Material was no problem to Muddy then. It seemed to pour out of him.

117

I used to go along and just make up stuff. I had me plenty of songs made up.
I made up all of 'em—"Long Distance Call," "Sittin' Here Drinkin'," "Mean
Red Spider," "Gypsy Woman," "Little Annie Mae," "Little General,"
"Honey Bee," "Sad Letter," "Louisiana Blues"—I made up all that stuff.
I could go along—in two hours time I had a song wrote. It just come
to me.

And it came to him both from the past in Mississippi and the present in
Chicago.

> *Lord I wish I was a catfish*
> *Swimmin' in the deep blue sea.*
> *I would have all you good lookin' women*
> *Fishin'*
> *After me, sho' 'nuff, after me*
>   *sho' 'nuff, after me*
>   *oh lord, oh lord,*
>   *sho' 'nuff*
>
> *I went to my baby's house*
> *And I sat down on her stairs,*
> *She said, "Come on in now Muddy,*
>   *know my husband's left*
>   *sho' 'nuff, just done left*
>   *sho' 'nuff, just done left*
>   *oh lord,*
>   *oh well, oh well*
>
> *Well my mother told my father*
> *Just before I was born*
> *I got a boy-child comin'*
> *Gonna be,*
> *He's gonna be a rolling stone*
> *Sho' 'nuff, he's a rolling stone*

BOSSMAN MUDDY WATERS

Oh well, he's a
Oh well, he's a
Oh well, he's a . . .*

Sometimes it was almost like preaching, Muddy by himself molding his voice to the lyrics. Other times it was more open, using the band, and especially Walter, to answer and support his voice.

You say you love me darlin',
Please call me on the phone sometime.
You say you love me darlin',
Please call me on the phone sometime.
When I hear your voice,
Eases my worried mind.

One of these days,
I'm gonna show you how nice a man can be.
One of these days, baby,
I'm gonna show you how nice a man can be.
I'm gonna buy you a brand new Cadillac
If you'll only say some good words about me.

Hear my phone ringin',
Sounds like a long distance call.
Hear my phone ringin',
Sounds like a long distance call.
When I picked up my receiver,
Party said, "Another mule's been kickin' in your stall."*†

119

On the early records I worked with just a bass and myself. They were trying to make a Lightning Hopkins out of me. But when I had Little Walter and Jimmy Rodgers, and Baby Face Leroy with me, they came to see that I sounded better with a little group. If I had stayed where I was I would have stayed like Lightning Hopkins—an old-time blues cat—which I would love to be. But I took the old-time music and brought it up to date—you've got to stay alive with it. You need to work. With a band I could play in clubs, for dances, concerts—anything. I am still an old-time singer, but I brought it out more.

I brought time to Chicago on blues. A lot of blues was played years and years ago—some of the best blues you ever did hear in your life—but they didn't have no time with them. The time is the key thing to it. Robert Johnson and Sonny Boy Williamson had it in their music. Their blues was like a clock. That's what I really like. I don't care what you sing, I think you can put some time with it. The big drop after beat on the drum formed the foundation of my blues. Nothing fancy—just a straight heavy beat with it.

I had records, records, records, records before I traveled. I stayed right here in Chicago playing those clubs. After a while we had so many people it was like a ball game, we'd have so many cars where I played at.

During these years, 1947–1952, the group stayed pretty much together. It was Muddy, Little Walter, and Jimmy Rodgers, with Willie Dixon coming in for record sessions to help out on bass. The music was gradually developing, taking shape, becoming a style. Willie Dixon describes how they would work at the early sessions.

With Muddy we started to put a beat behind the music and make definite rhythm patterns. I was playing the bass on almost all of Muddy's early things, and we tried to set up a melodic pattern to match the rhythm, and this gave those songs the feeling we wanted. And after doing many of them it became a style. And people liked it better with this solid blues beat.

Muddy too was aware that he was creating a style, and that his records would be the way people would identify him, but he could never allow himself to become the prisoner of his records. He wanted his music to stay alive and keep moving.

Talking about making that sound and bringing it out—which you don't have on record. I like to do it like that. After the record got out, then I start doing it different. I think I plays it better, more freer. 'Cause when you're in the studio, you know, you're kinda uptight. But I still play 'em so that people still know that I am Muddy Waters, you know. But this playing note for note and all, I don't do nothing like that. I think I can play 'em better off the bandstand than I do on records. Some nights, though, seems like nothing's happening. Even when I was really drinking liquor. I couldn't make it happen. Just one of those nights. Then there comes some nights when you hit the bandstand, you got everything going.

By 1952 things were going pretty well. Clubs would be packed where Muddy played. The records were doing well in Chicago and, as a result of air play on the "colored" radio stations, they were starting to move in other cities as well. Some of the success began to rub off on Walter.

He was with me from forty-seven to fifty-two—five good years. That's when we made all the old good-time records. Then he went on his own with his first hit, "Juke." We made it. See, that used to be our theme song, going on the stage and coming off. And we put it on record and it went. I picked up Junior Wells then. He had a little band with Fred Below and Lewis and Dave Meyers called "The Four Aces." So Walter picked up the band and I brought Junior out of the band with me, you know. So when Walter made up his mind to get his own thing, then I brought Junior right in with me—kept rolling.

"Kept rolling" is a pretty good description of the way Muddy handled this and all subsequent personnel changes. It came from a deep confidence in

himself as a leader capable of incorporating new men into his band, teaching
them his music, and bringing out whatever potential they had.

**When a new man comes into the group you first try to learn him the hard
things that you do, 'cause them other things that you do, well, if you know how
to play blues then you don't have no problem. Now I got some things that if
you ain't in the band, I doubt if you can do it—"Just To Be With You,"
"Just Make Love To Me," those kind of songs. You'll have a little scuffle and
you'll be in the band with 'em, you know. Because they got so many funny,
tricky things in 'em, you know. Half-notes or something, you know, you just
can't walk out of the streets and play that. Not the way I recorded it.**
**Every kind of music you can name got a lot of talent in there, but there got
to be some masters and some sidemen behind. There's a lot of 'em can play
some, can play good, but they ain't deep enough, know what I mean—they
ain't got that tone deep enough. When you play blues, you may play blues,
but you ain't got no tone; but you see blues, it's tone—deep tone with a
heavy beat.**
**After Little Walter left I would try to get them to put in some things that was
going on. But there was a lot of things that they couldn't exactly put in there,
you know. But you can't stop because one member drops out. You must keep
going. Old saying—"one monkey don't stop no show, slows it down."**

It happened that just as Walter left, Otis Spann joined the band. Muddy calls
Otis his brother, and they were that close until Otis's untimely death in April
of 1970. Having him in the band for so many years through various personnel
changes eased the transition periods and helped give the band a definite
identity and continuity, as well as a bigger, fuller sound that Muddy wanted
in his music.

Another change was the piano. In forty-nine or fifty I made "Screamin' and

Otis Spann *(Photo: David Ga*

Cryin' " with Little Johnny Jones on piano. I didn't use it again until Otis Spann came out of the army in fifty-three. I got him back into the music business. We had fooled around some before that, but we really got together then in fifty-three. If you get that piano in there you get a whole full bed of background music.

Before they had pianos and guitars together like Leroy Carr and Scrapper Blackwell, but that wasn't a big sound. I developed that. I kept that backbeat on the drums plus full action on the guitar and harmonica and the piano in the back, then you've got a big sound. It was in my head. Nobody ever told me about it. I had it in my head that the piano always was a blues instrument and belonged with my blues.

Spann and I had a thing together. I felt very close to him. He'd do things right to fit the song. 'Course, he's on all the records. He knows how they go and everything and he could kick 'em off and the band follow.

That's where you have a lot of advantage—when you've got a guy with you that can play and stays with you and he knows any moves you want to make. That makes a good band. He fills those cracks and holes up. He takes care of the business for you.

Having Otis in the band gave it the sound Muddy was looking for. The piano would be there under the voice, the guitar, and the harmonica, helping with the rhythm, embellishing the lyric, and answering to Muddy's slide guitar. Muddy took Spann's virtuoso blues piano playing and made it fit with his songs "like a glove." Like Walter's harp playing and Dixon's bass lines, Spann's piano sound became identified with Muddy Waters's blues band style. Just about the time Spann joined Muddy, Willie Dixon persuaded Muddy that he had more to offer him than a good bass line on a record.

I met Muddy Waters sometime in forty-seven or forty-eight. There was plenty going on then. Just about all of the places on the South Side was considered blues spots, and there was a lot of different groups in one spot or another, and they was all playing blues. Muddy was working over on Wentworth Avenue, him and Little Walter. In fact, Walter had just joined him. I used to go over there and sit around with them, and all the time I had been trying to write songs, but most of the songs I wrote I had never done anything with. Every so often I would ask him, "Why don't you try some of the songs that I write?" He said, "If you've got some good ones, I'll try it." So a little later Muddy was getting ready to record for the Chess Company, and he asked me to come down and play bass on this session. That's when they had the Aristocrat Recording Company before it came to be Chess. The first tune I gave Muddy was "Hoochie Coochie Man." I wrote it for him, and it turned out to be a big hit. That was around fifty-three.

If ever a song was written for a man to sing, "Hoochie Coochie Man" was written for Muddy Waters.

The gypsy woman told my mother,
Before I was born
You got a boy-child comin'
Gonna be a son of a gun,
He's gonna make pretty women
Jump and shout,
Then the world's gonna know what it's all about,
'Cause you know I'm here,
Everybody knows I'm here.
You know I'm the hoochie coochie man,
Everybody knows I'm here.

I got a black cat bone,
I got a mojo too,
I got the John the Conqueroo,
I'm gonna mess with you.
I'm gonna make you girls
Lead me by my hand
Then the world's gonna know,

I'm the hoochie coochie man
'Cause you know I'm here,
Everybody knows I'm here.
You know I'm the hoochie coochie man,
Everybody knows I'm here.

On the seventh hour
On the seventh day
On the seventh month
The seven doctors say,
He was born for good luck,
And that you'll see,
I got seven-hundred dollars,
Don't you mess with me,
'Cause you know I'm here,
Everybody knows I'm here.
You know I'm the hoochie coochie man,
*Everybody knows I'm here.**

And if they didn't know it then, they soon would.
Between Willie's songs and Muddy's own, Muddy firmly established himself
as the top man on the Chicago blues scene. Chicago finally had become
his home, and the South Side was his territory. He worked it hard and long,
nearly every night of every week in the year.

**When I was going here we worked nearly every week in the year. Didn't miss
no weeks unless I was sick. A lot of nights in those clubs—hard work. And
we didn't have them kinda nice hours in those clubs. Mostly we had the late
hour license. Four o'clock in the morning—three and four and five o'clock in**

the morning. On Saturday night go to about five. Summertime it was daybreak. Go there in the day and leave in the day—next day.

With the band that included Little Junior Wells on harp and Spann on piano, Muddy began to move out of Chicago a little—but not too far: one nighters

left to right: Muddy Waters, unknown, Otis Spann, Henry Strong, Elgin Evans, Jimmy Rogers

in Nashville or St. Louis, then straight back to those Chicago clubs. The personnel situation didn't stay settled for too long.

127

Junior went into the Army; then I brought Big Walter with me—Walter Horton. Junior didn't stay in there no time. He went in and run right off. He stayed AWOL. But, you see, I had to get another harp blower, cause he'd go there and run off and come back and they'd be looking for him and he'd be scared to come out to the club. So Big Walter Horton stayed with me a pretty good little while.

Now Big Walter was a heavy harp blower. When he was with me he was very heavy. They didn't butt in up on him too fast. He cut one session with me. And Junior cut one session with me.

After Walter Horton I got this boy Henry Strong. His nickname was "Pot" —he got killed right over here on Greenwood. Then I got George Smith with me, but he was looking for, you know, his own thing.

Then back to Junior Wells again. Junior had got his dishonorable discharge. Then he messed up again. He left me in Tampa, Florida, and came home. So I picked up James Cotton in Memphis. I had a driver then who knew him from when he was a kid. He found him for me and we brought him on to Chicago with us.

He stayed with me about twelve years. He was young when he came with me —young, didn't have no ties, just blowing it. I got him fixed up, seasoned him up. He stayed with me a pretty long time. A lot of places I carried him at— I carried him to Florida—I had to send for Junior to finish the week out with me. People said, "Why don't you get the other little harp blower?" A lot of places I'd go they wanted me I should have Junior with me you know. After Cotton got known, they quit worrying 'bout it. He went to blowing.

When Muddy talks about these years that little phrase, "He was looking for his own thing," crops up all the time.

Any sideman you got in your band—he's working for the day to come when he's strong enough to go on his own. You can't fault him for that, 'cause everybody wants to make a star. Like I did when I was a sideman; I was working for that day to come when I could hit it for myself, you know. But I felt like I had it. I never doubted myself one time I didn't have it. I knowed that. Just knowed I had it. All I had to do was get a chance to let it out 'cause there ain't many peoples sings like me and ain't got it, you know what I mean (ha, ha, ha). I just had that feeling I had it. I know I got it (to myself) all I need is somebody to give me a break and put a record out on me. But, you know, the one that can't sing at all, he feels the same way. Feels like he's got it. Feels like if he can get a record out then he'll have a hit. That's why we get a lot of records out that don't do nothing. Because everybody just can't cut through it. And to get a blues out there, you've got to sing.

Having sidemen leave is a fact of life for every leader. You get someone good, bring him along, give him a chance, then he leaves and you start all over again. It's a rare leader who will really let the process go on without feeling threatened.

James Cotton, Junior, even Paul Butterfield—they definitely got some of my stuff. Ain't no maybe about it, they're definitely coming across with some of my music. They've maybe learned something else now, but when they began, they came across with my stuff, they was coming all the way across with it. Amongst the blues bands, most every night they play—they can't miss me. They gotta hit somewhere where I've been. I'm the old grandfather of 'em. I set the pattern for 'em. They got a little of me, then advanced out and picked up other stuff, but I'm in there somewhere.
Take Howlin' Wolf, you know, no one's passed through his band. I don't know of one man who's passed through his band. And I've started quite a few of them. One thing might have a little to do with it—it's not everything— but guys don't give their members enough opportunity. They holds 'em back and I don't. I let the whole thing work. Sing. See who likes you. I try to expose my band. Not only Wolf but a whole lot of them don't do that. They want everything for themself. They're jealous. They're afraid one of the band members may beat them to the point that night. But when one of my band members goes over big, I really like it. I enjoy it. That makes me feel good because, number one, when they go home they ain't gonna say, "The band was good"—ha, ha, ha—gonna say that Muddy Waters' band was good, know

129

what I mean? A lot of the people ain't like that; I don't know what's wrong with them. I can't figure it out to save my neck. Why they don't want to give the band members a break. They want to sing sometimes. Some of 'em can sing good. Some of 'em can't. I let 'em all try. I got some in my band, they can't sing, but I let 'em try. They think they can, so I give it to 'em—go on, sing a couple of songs. He feels good behind that, you know. Everybody wants to make a star; you can be way back in the backfield playing sideman, but in your mind you wish you was up front. So give 'em a chance. Don't hold people back. There might have been some people came through Wolf's band if he had let 'em went on. I know Wolf, 'cause we've been playing together at clubs here in town. I let my band play up there half an hour before I go up there. But as soon as his band plays the theme song he's on his way. Ha, ha, ha. You can't take everything with you, you know. You have to get your little bit and give somebody else some of it. And another thing. When I do come on after another singer you can see that somebody's up there. See I ain't worried about none of my band running me out. Just let 'em please their own mind, and they feel more freer working.

And through it all there is much that cannot be directly communicated to those coming into the band. Through some mysterious process they have to "know." What is it that distinguishes a good player from a bad one, a brilliant player from a good one? It's more than just notes. And what does a leader do with someone who doesn't seem to get it?

A lot of other people will play for you—have good reputations—and you find out they're not on it. And you're not really an outstanding musician when you get on the guy to his face that, "so and so and so on." There are some people who qualify to be told. Just like you have a guy you think he can cover all the holes for you and then when he plays with you a couple of songs he don't do nothing for you. Some people will tell him, "Well, man, you ain't playing nothing." But I can't do that. You got to have a man behind you.

Muddy and Band Relaxing *(Photo: David G*

'Cause I can't cover up for myself too good and slide at the same time. And I want somebody behind me to keep the ball rolling, while I'm doing my thing, and I've been with a lot of 'em couldn't do it. I don't know. Just a simple thing they had to do and they couldn't do it. I don't know why. They do it another way. I guess they do it the way they learned to do it or feel like doing it, I don't know. But looks like my blues is so simple to play and then again it's hard. There's a lot of people say, "Man, anybody can play that." Then they get up to play and can't play. Looks like to me my blues is so simple to play, so easy to play, and then I have a lot of guys say, "Man, I can't play, you play with it." Nothing but a twelve bar blues and he can't play. I don't understand it. Maybe I do it the wrong way, 'cause I'm kind of a delay singer, maybe. There's a lot of guys, if he ain't on the beat, he can't play it. But you've got to learn to play behind the beat a little. I've played with John Lee Hooker. Ha, ha. I follow him. When he changes, I change. If he don't never change, I don't never change, I just keep hitting it. A lot of people can't hear. They got a bad ear. I can hear most anything on the bandstand. I'm lucky. I got a good ear. 'Cause that's what I works by—my ear. I can hear anything up there, mostly—if you fumble, I gotcha. Some men are so hard to keep in line, I almost give it up. You tell 'em how you want it done and they still can't do it. Man, I've had good guitar players I can't learn my bass line in rehearsal. Show 'em what I wanted them to do—but because I'm not on the beat, they can't do it. And mighty few good blues players you see is on the beat.

By the mid-fifties the band had settled down into a solid groove. Spann was on piano and Cotton was on harmonica and this was to be the heart of Muddy's band for the next ten years. At the same time, black music was building a solid circuit in the South. Muddy's records were getting played on "colored" radio stations throughout the region from Florida over to Texas, and he finally decided that he'd better get an agent and start playing out on the road while it was hot.

'Bout fifty-four it started to blooming. I finally got a booking agent who talked me into traveling. 'Cause I wasn't going nowhere. I was doing all right in

BOSSMAN MUDDY WATERS

Chicago and I said, "I don't want to travel." But we went out.
Had about thirty-one one-nighters with Sarah Vaughn, Al Hibbler,
Moonglows, Red Prysock, Nappy Brown—and, boy, we killed 'em. Me and
Nappy Brown murdered them people all around through Texas, Louisiana,
Alabama. We just really murdered them. That's when Sarah was a big star
down in that Southern country. Had a Greyhound for the sidemen and a
Greyhound for the stars. Had me sitting up there with the stars. I said, "I
don't dig this." Sometimes I'd get on the bus with the sidemen. They had fun
on there. They'se playing cards, drinking. I don't feel like no star anyway.
Forget the star, just plain Muddy Waters. I was the boss of my
little outfit.

But the tours with the "stars" were not the usual thing. Mostly it was clubs,
dances, one-nighters—a lot of it in rough areas for not a lot of money—three
to five hundred dollars a night. Keeping six men alive on the road wasn't
easy or safe.

It's a hard way to make a living—you better believe it. A lot of people think
this is something easy. But this is hard, dangerous. You run down the highway
every day and it's very dangerous. We've been so lucky with it—good
drivers. I'd always be cautious about it, you know. I'd keep 'em down with
that speed, when I was around. When I'd be flying or something they might
go on up there. But I keep 'em down with that speed. And be sure you obey
signs and obey that weather. Ice on the ground, come out of there—starts
a'raining, cut that speed—if it say sixty-five miles an hour, don't pay it no
attention; the highway is wet, just try to live.
People definitely don't understand how hard it is sometimes. They don't
know nothing. They just see you. If you ain't on it, you're through. You might
have just driven all day to make it and you're so tired you can't make it. But
you're through. Every time you go on-stage somebody's looking for you to do
your best. Do top-notch entertainment. Sometimes you go up there, you're
half sick. But other times things can just click off. But you don't get that
feeling every time. So no matter what, you've got to be professional about it
and do it.

Despite the difficulties, though, by the end of the fifties the band was into a pretty set routine, alternating the one-nighters in the South on the road with a few weeks at a club in Chicago. That might have been it for Muddy for a long time. It suited him. He was established. He kept his band working. His records were selling steadily. He could pay his bills and live comfortably. He had bought a house on Lake Park Avenue on the South Side where he lived with his wife Geneva and their children. He was working hard, but it was worth it, and he was happy with the way things had turned out. He had come a long way from Stovall's plantation.

But things were happening in the music business that were to affect Muddy's life and enable him to come closer than he had dared hope to becoming "internationally known." It started around nineteen fifty-three and fifty-four when Fats Domino hit the record world with such tunes as "Ain't That A Shame" and "Please Don't Leave Me." After a diet of Patti Page and Rosemary Clooney, Fats's sound was another whole world—the world of "rhythm and blues." After Fats it was Little Richard with his supercharged "Tutti Frutti." Then there were the mellower sounds of Ivory Joe Hunter, Clyde McPhatter, and the gutsy sound of Earl Bostic and his saxophone. Then came the countless groups: the Coasters, the Drifters, the Moonglows, and the Clovers.

Suddenly black music was being played on white radio. It was an explosion. It affected the black market as well as the white, because the record companies started releasing more singles and started putting out albums of artists who would have received limited exposure before. Black radio stations (white owned) were starting to compete with white. For the first time, the white market for black music was being discovered and fully exploited.

This was the time when Muddy Waters began traveling, and he too became part of the "rhythm and blues" world. However, he didn't get outside of the black market because his music wasn't really danceable, and that was the real thing behind the popularity of rhythm and blues or "rock and roll," as it was coming to be called. Almost every week a new dance was born. A prime catalyst in spreading the new dances was the television show "American Bandstand," starring Dick Clark, who was one of the first to really understand the enormous implications of this injection of black music into American popular music and what it meant for the "youth market." Soon it was time

for "The Twist" with Chubby Checker, and Chuck Berry became the
epitome of the dancing fool.
Somewhere along the line "rhythm and blues" had become "rhythm." The
blues were still in Chicago and those little clubs throughout the South.
Muddy Waters's music was too rough, too real and solid, to get swept into
the national frenzy. He didn't try to change his style of music. It was the only
music he could play. He had grown up with it as a young man. He had
adapted it to meet the requirements of playing in clubs, but the soul of the
music was unchanged, and the sound was still that raw, muscular Delta sound
that seemed to fit life in Chicago so well. The main thing that distinguished
it from most of the popular music, apart from the slow, heavy beat, was its
personal quality, the intimacy that Muddy strove to establish with his
audience.

**A blues singer—he'll never get rich. He never gets rich. He's still hustling and
scuffling and he's talking to the people and enjoying his own self. He ain't
only talking to himself. He's talking to the other people too. I sing what
people have been upon or what someday they might come upon.
My music did a lot of things for peoples. Many times people have told me it
did. Plenty times. Yeah, I've heard 'em tell me my music changed them.
Once even a guy played my record over and over and over. Walked out in
the street and a car killed him walking the highway. So I've had a lot that's
happened with my music. And women have told me, "You caused me and my
husband to separate." And women have told me, "You have brought me and
my husband together." So I don't know what the hell to do—ha, ha, ha—this
is stuff I don't know what's happening with my music. You never know
who's listening.
In Frisco a young man says to me that I done saved him. He said that he had
given up until he heard my records. In the back of my head I wondered. He
said he was down and going wrong, and then he heard my blues and got back
on the track.**

In a sense, this life wasn't too far from being a preacher, the other occupation

Photo: David Gahr

Muddy had considered for himself when he was young. He was up there, leading his band, bringing them with him, and talking to his audience with his voice and his guitar. He was talking about troubles and, in the very act of telling about them, overcoming them by the strength of his singing and playing. When it was working right it could be powerful and would make the long hours, the hard work—everything—seem worth it.

Once upon a time I had the blues bad. I couldn't pay my rent, couldn't pay my light bill. Today I can pay my light bill, can pay my rent—and I still got the blues. It's from the heart. That's my religion. Sometimes I get so happy singing the blues that I jump right up on the bandstand. That's when I get my feeling in.

It seemed that if Muddy didn't change his music drastically, the popular music world might just leave him alone in Chicago talking to his own people. However, by the end of the fifties there were some indications that the outside world was starting to move in Muddy's direction. The first stirrings came, strangely enough, from England.

By the mid-fifties there was a strong folk music revival going in England. Little clubs sprang up where traditional performers could be heard. At first the emphasis was on the music of the British Isles, but it soon expanded to include the mountain music of the Appalachians and the blues. Their interest was in strictly traditional, old-time music, however; not in the modern electrified music. Muddy was invited to come over in 1958, and went just as he was, amplifier and all. It was a shocker for the folk fans.

When I first went to England in fifty-eight I didn't have no idea what was going on. I was touring with Chris Barber—a dixieland band. They thought I was a Big Bill Broonzy—which I wasn't. I had my amplifier and Spann and I was going to do a Chicago thing; we opened up in Leeds, England. I was definitely too loud for them then. The next morning we were in the headlines of the paper—"Screaming Guitar and Howling Piano." That was when they were into the folk thing before the Rolling Stones.

Confusing as it might have been to Muddy, the response to his music in England wasn't confined to the concerts and clubs. There was something else

going on at the same time at another social level. American rock and roll had
invaded. Elvis, Bill Haley and the Comets, Jerry Lee Lewis had all come
over and were tearing up the kids. These were tough working-class kids as
opposed to the more intellectual types who were involved in the folk revival.
In the wake of these "rockers" many young English kids started steeping
themselves in American music. As in America, English popular music had
been pretty bland, and this new music with its heavy beat and excitement
seemed to meet a need. A few of these kids began to hear some of the
bluesmen who were coming over on the folk circuit. Little magazines began
to publish articles and discographies about blues artists. Record companies
responded by reissuing old records. In rooms around London, Liverpool,
Manchester, and Bristol, Muddy Waters was on the phonograph. The seeds
were settling and taking root.

Meanwhile, back in the USA, things were beginning to move too. One of the
major musical events of the day was the Newport Jazz Festival. By the
summer of 1960, the festival was at its height and was pointing the way to the
future in the presentation of popular music. The audience was a wide range
of jazz fans, black and white, mostly middle class, with a heavy helping of
white college students. Producer George Wein decided that the festival
should include a blues program in acknowledgment of the debt of jazz to the
blues. Muddy and his band closed the program, and the reception was
overwhelming—a standing ovation. These weren't people from Mississippi
or poor blacks from the urban ghetto, but the music said something to them
in a way that the more sophisticated music on the programs hadn't. It was
another indication of which way the wind was blowing.

Aside from these occasional forays into the outside world, Muddy's routine
kept him in the clubs in Chicago and on the road in the South. On his home
ground there was no question about his place on the scene. The young
guitar player, Buddy Guy, up from New Orleans and trying to find his way
in the blues scene, tells of his first meeting with Muddy:

**I really dig Muddy. First time I met him was the crucial time when I was
first here. He drove up to the 708 Club and I was on there and Muddy sent in
and said, "Tell that little old boy I said come on out here."**

I said, "Muddy Waters? I'll go out in a minute just to get a chance to meet him." I walked out and he was sitting in a station wagon in the front seat, so I attempted to get in the back.
"Don't get in the back. Get in the front." So I got in the front. And he's sitting up there eating a baloney sandwich. "Go ahead on, get you some baloney, make you a sandwich."
So I started thinking, This cat here is better than I thought he was. I thought he was going to be after saying, "Look man, you know, I'm Muddy Waters," but he was down to earth and I thought, "Wow, what else can you ask for?"
He says, "First of all, I want to know where're you from."
"I'm from Louisiana."
"I should have figured that, but I thought you was from Mississippi, boy. I'm from Mississippi."
We've been tight ever since, and I really love him for that.

With Muddy's blessing, Buddy was happy to join the burgeoning blues scene in Chicago. On top were Muddy, Howlin' Wolf and Little Walter. Then there was Little Junior Wells with whom Buddy was to team up, Otis Rush, Magic Sam, Willis Maybon, Hound Dog Taylor, Big Walter Horton, J. B. Hutto, Little Milton, and many others who could be found at Pepper's or Theresa's or any of a number of clubs and lounges that featured blues one or two nights a week. It was a lively time, and Muddy was enjoying it, but he still wondered about the outside world, and if his music would ever be accepted there.
In 1962 he got another call to come to England. If they wanted him he was going to go, but he had no high hopes about the trip. When he arrived he was totally unprepared for what happened.

I went back—took my acoustic with me—and everybody's hollering—"Where's your amplifier?" I said, "When I was here before they didn't like my stuff." But those English groups had picked up on my stuff and went wild with it. I said, "I never know what's going on." A bunch of those young kids came around. They could play. They'd pick up my guitar and fool with it.

Then the Rolling Stones came out named after my song, you know, and recorded "Just Make Love to Me" and the next I knew they were out there. And that's how people in the States really got to know who Muddy Waters was.

Soon after returning to the States, Muddy got another call. This time it was from his agency, Shaw Artists. They had a job for him to play up in Boston at the Jazz Workshop. This, too, was something new. When he got there, he met the man who had booked him, Bob Messinger. Messinger was a jazz fan who knew of blues artists primarily through records. He had a hunch that someone like Muddy might do well on the basis of what had happened at Newport, so he tracked him down through Shaw Artists who had been booking his one-nighters. It was the first booking of this sort they had received. They felt that Muddy would want to do it, and they sent him up to Boston. Messinger remembers the time vividly:

Opening night came and Muddy showed up with a six-piece band, and we were told he was coming with five pieces. So I asked him how he could do it. He said, "These boys wanted to make a trip. It's the first time a Chicago blues band has been called to a city in the East for a long time."
Along about the third night he asked me, "What exactly do you do? Do you own this club or are you the booker or what?"
And I said, "I'm the house booker, and I've been looking for you for some time, and I think I can book other dates for you."
And he said, "Well, look, man, I've never had a manager, but maybe I could use one. I get a good record on the colored stations every once in a while, and when I do I go out down South for some one-nighters; then I come back home and play Pepper's for a while until I go out again. But I ain't got no white work like this for a long while."
So I said, "Well, I think the white market's going to be ready for you, Muddy. Why don't we work out something?"

Willie Dixon *(Photo: David Ga*

140

JAMES ROONEY

Workshop at Newport Folk Festival

BOSSMAN MUDDY WATERS

(Photo: David Gahr)

"Do you want me to sign a paper or something?"
I said, "No, let's just shake hands and see how it works out. If we like each
other and get along okay, then maybe we'll have some paper."

Later Muddy did send Bob a letter authorizing him to sign contracts, but
they never have had a formal management contract.

I don't think I would ever want a piece of paper with Muddy. It would limit
our relationship. I'm closer to Muddy than I am to my own father. To me
Muddy is the older man I look up to and respect in my life. And most of the
reasons I respect Muddy haven't a damn thing to do with music. I've
watched him handle that band and that incredible melange of personalities
he's assembled. With no temper or pettyness he is the boss, and that's it.

Buoyed by his success in England and the interest shown by Messinger, Muddy
returned to Chicago to see what was going to happen. It was slow but sure
in coming, and Messinger was patiently nursing it along.

The white jobs kept coming little by little. For a few years there I had a
policy of never turning down a white school date. Whatever money we got,
we played it. Of course, things began to pick up significantly after the Beatles
and the Stones hit. One of the first things the Beatles said when they got here
was that they wanted to go see Muddy Waters and Bo Diddley.
Some reporter said, "Where's that?"
They laughed and said, "Don't you know who your own famous people
are here?"

It was all a bit puzzling to Muddy—the way the message had to come to
America from England about him, but he was glad to get it any
way he could.

BOSSMAN MUDDY WATERS

After the Rolling Stones and Beatles it opened up for me for both black and white. Before that the audience wasn't exposed too much to the blues. To get to the white people then I think you had to do it on your own strength, just like Fats Domino got to 'em 'cause they loved what he was doing. He really played their type of shit. But my kind of music had to be exposed to 'em. And it wasn't exposed to 'em until after the Rolling Stones and the Beatles. That's a funny damn thing. Had to get somebody from out of another country to let my white kids over here know where we stand. They're crying for bread and got it in their backyard. They got some of the best blues singers that ever lived right here in the United States—ha, ha, ha—there's nobody else, you know. So that's a terrible thing. But I guess it took that to wake 'em up. They sure ain't got no real good blues singers in England. But they got some heck of a players there—guitars, every other thing—piano, organ, everything.

Even in Chicago things were starting to change. Muddy was starting to see some young white faces where he was playing. Some of the kids at the University of Chicago were beginning to discover the music in the bars on the South Side near the school and were getting into playing it. The man in the middle of this activity, however, wasn't at the university. He was a tough, hustling, Irish kid from Chicago who didn't have to study to understand the blues. His name was Paul Butterfield.
Butterfield felt the urge to play the blues as soon as he heard the music. The blues talked to him about his own growing up on the streets of Chicago, and he started really getting into the blues as a teenager in the late fifties. The harmonica became his instrument, and Little Walter and James Cotton his masters. By the early sixties Paul was welcome to sit in at sessions around town in various lounges. He became the natural leader for the university students who were starting to get into the music themselves. It was only a matter of time before he formed a band with two of the most talented young guitar players on the scene—Mike Bloomfield and Elvin Bishop. For rhythm he had two young bluesmen—Jerome Arnold and Sam Lay.
Word began to filter out of Chicago in the spring of 1965 that there was a young harp blower in Chicago who had a hell of a band. The rumor was

confirmed when the band came to New York and woke up the folk fans at the Cafe Au Go Go. The next stop was the Newport Folk Festival, which had featured older bluesmen like Son House and Skip James, but which had shied away from presenting any blues bands, unsure as to whether or not it was "folk music." It is ironic to note that this barrier was broken not by Muddy Waters or Howlin' Wolf or any one of the Chicago bluesmen with a direct link to the roots of the music, but by a third-generation band which drew its inspiration from Muddy, Walter, and Wolf.

Be that as it may, the excitement caused by the Butterfield Blues Band at Newport was considerable, and it opened up the world of the blues—Chicago blues—to thousands of kids. Soon, other white groups came out of Chicago— Seigal-Schwall, Charley Musselwhite, Steve Miller. And the groups that had been there all along—Howlin' Wolf, Junior Wells, Buddy Guy. Everybody had the blues. Folk coffee houses like the Club 47 in Cambridge and the Cafe Au Go Go in New York began featuring the different blues bands. Muddy Waters found himself suddenly thrust into an all-white, middle-class, student world. It was a world that had been denied to him because of his background, and now he found its children coming to him, all wearing Levis, it seemed, with long hair, doing their best to look "folky" and to hide their middle-class upbringing. They reached out for his music and embraced it, responding to its strength, its vitality, its authority. It was real, and that reality of Muddy Waters's music gave them something they hadn't found in the suburbs.

As a result of this incredible interest in Chicago blues, Muddy found himself working more and more away from Chicago. The jobs were in coffee houses, colleges, the Newport Folk Festival, the Monterey Jazz Festival. With the exception of some all-blues shows at the Apollo Theater in New York, Muddy was doing almost no work for black audiences. He was happy to be working as much as he was, but inside he would wonder about his own people and their relation to his music.

There ain't enough of my peoples trying to get interested in playing the blues and that's what really keeps me kind of worried about it, 'cause they can do it, you know.

Maybe when these young ones are together—another few years older, they
might turn 'round a little bit. Teenagers, they're going to that James Brown
beat, but when they get up in their twenties they'll probably turn 'round and
get another thing. They can't stay there. They got to go someway. It may
not be to the blues, but they'll go some other way.

To many young blacks, the blues is a part of their past they'd rather forget.
"Soul" is what's happening. You can dance to it, strut to it, get with it, and
walk tall to it. James Brown, Wilson Pickett, Sam & Dave, Joe Tex, The
Temptations, all speak to the young. They wear the hippest clothes, do fast-
paced shows with precision dance routines, and do their best to bring everyone
up to a fever pitch. Dance becomes a form of escape from the ghetto while
at the same time affirming one's black soul with a step that whites can only
feebly imitate.
In comparison, Muddy's band and music doesn't seem very exciting. You see
six men dressed in different suits, looking like they've spent their lives in
clubs, laying down a slow, heavy beat, with Muddy up front singing the blues,
getting deep into the blues, his body rocking slightly, his face wincing as he
barks out the verses. It is not an escape from anything. It's the way things are,
and for most young blacks, they've had enough reality to last them awhile.
Muddy is fully aware of the bad image of the bluesman.

You see when you say "blues" you know what the average guy is looking for
when he comes in—half slouching, raggedy, bottle of wine in your pocket. I
wasn't that kind of blues singer. I stayed sharp. If I had anything it was some
of the best. That's the kind of blues singer I am. I wasn't a cat to come in
with a big bottle of wine in my pocket and talking loud. Not me. When I
wanted a drink it was Chivas Regal. I was never that type of man who'd have
a great big quart of wine laying back of the amplifier. I am an intelligent
blues singer. I sing deep, Down South blues, straight out of the bottom. But
I made myself classy with it. People have told me I should be preaching
looking as I do. They'd say, "I looked to see a man with a pair of overalls on,
cap pulled down over his ears, and just as drunk as he could be." And I

said, "Not me, baby. I'm sharp. I've got my mohair. Not me. That's for the birds." I'm a gentleman with my blues singing. If I tell you I'm going to do something, I'm going to do it. I ain't gonna lie to you. This is my business. And I'm very intelligent with it. You don't have to have a white face to be a gentleman and up to date with what you're doing. You can be black, brown, or any color, but you've got to carry yourself in a way that people know that you're it. They might say I can't play, or can't sing, but, damn it, they'll say I'm a gentleman.

I don't think you should be down on the blues or any other kind of music as long as it's done right. I don't dig it, man, I'm sorry. I may be wrong, but no music should be criticized. Jazz, dixieland, blues—whatever it is. If you can play it good, just say, whatever it is, "He's playing it." I don't think you should criticize. I've got my thing. I do my thing. Count does his thing. Duke does his thing. And we do it good. We are creators. That's it. Other people who try to do what we do never will match up with us.

If I hadn't come to Chicago, I don't know who would have kept it alive. And we'll see who'll keep it alive after I've done made it through the scene. Most of them are into another scene now. We can't live always. Who's gonna take it? It's gotta come from the black people. They're ducking. They're running from it.

If the blacks weren't playing the blues, the young whites certainly were. Paul Butterfield's band spun off two other groups, one headed by Mike Bloomfield, the other by Elvin Bishop. In the wake of the Beatles and the Stones, a slew of English groups arose, at the head of which was John Mayall and the Bluesbreakers. Then came Eric Clapton, Stevie Winwood, Jimmy Page, Alvin and Rick Lee, Jeff Beck, and many others. The singing on the whole was a strangely distorted imitation of something between Muddy and Howlin' Wolf. Sheer volume and a thundering beat made any subtlety out of the question. Only Mayall and the young Chicagoans seemed to have any understanding of the range and depth of the blues, and it was still thin vocally. Be that as it may, these groups were phenomenally successful. By

o: David Gahr

the late sixties many of the groups were getting $10,000 or more per performance. Some of this was bound to rub off on Muddy. He was able to get more for a concert than in the past, but it was nowhere near what the white groups were getting. Bob Messinger had been right that he was going to be getting a lot of "white" jobs, but he hadn't predicted the incredible influx of barely professional, young, white musicians.

It's too easy for a well-schooled young white musician to cop all the licks and get the superficial part of it all down. It's not like jazz where the oil always floated on the water. You can separate the men from the boys pretty quickly there. But in the blues it's a problem, because you've got too many third-rate white musicians out there who don't belong, earning a living. Muddy Waters is a professional. He's been out there for thirty years. He put together a style of music—the Chicago blues band—and it would seem right that he should be getting his due in this blues revival.

Another disturbing factor in Muddy's career at this point was the direction Chess Records took with his records. Instead of letting Muddy do what he did best—sing the blues with his band—they decided that he had better update his music. The first attempt was to make him more of a "soul" singer to see if they could latch him onto that trend. The result was an album entitled *Muddy and Brass,* which sounded as if the two had never met. Muddy Waters was Muddy Waters, not B. B. King or James Brown. If the record company didn't recognize the differences, Muddy did.

B. B.'s got that squeezing sound. Man, that's a different country from me. My sound and his sound is the same as two different countries. 'Cause I'm not a squeeze man. That's what I try to keep my guitar players down with. Don't put too much B.B. on me. It don't mix. I'd rather for you to play big-four chords, you know. But if I give you a solo then you can go wild, you can do what you want to do. But behind me, don't put too much squeeze behind me. And the "soul" thing is a whole other country. My band can't cut through

that. They was got together for a different sound. It's plumb out of our field. Sometimes we go and play dance music. Well, we does it, but I ain't together there, you know. I can't play dance music. James Brown has got the band for dance music. I don't have it.

Undaunted, the company then decided that the psychedelic fad was what was really happening. That's what the white kids were into, and that's where Muddy's audience was now, so they did an album entitled, humorously enough, *Electric Mud*. The humor stopped with the title. Muddy was lost amid the fuzz-tones, the wah-wahs, and the nonstop drums. Muddy had gone along with it as an experiment, but musically it didn't make it.

When I made *Electric Mud* I couldn't play it on the bandstand. People would want to hear a number off the record and I'd have to make excuses about how I recorded with a studio band and my band has been so busy—blah, blah, blah—now what the hell do you have a record for you can't play it the first time it's out. I'm sick of that. That's out.
If you've got to have big amplifiers and wah-wahs and equipment to make your guitar say different things well, hell, you can't play no blues. Forget it. That guitar sounds just like a cat—meow—and the drums have a loping, busy beat.
I was looking at it a different way than the company. Quite naturally, I like a good selling record. That's what I'm in the business for, you know. But I was looking at it because I played for so many of these so-called hippies, that I thought probably I could reach them, you know. But maybe the company was looking at it for sales profit. It did sell big.

The only good album to come out of this period of experimentation (aside from excellent collections of earlier singles) was an album entitled *Fathers and Sons,* which brought Muddy and Spann together with Paul Butterfield and Mike Bloomfield, backed up by Buddy Miles, Sam Lay, and Duck Dunn. The difference between this and the other albums was that everyone played

Muddy's music, and they played it with feeling. It wasn't soul, it wasn't a freakout, it was the blues, and it said something about Muddy's relationship to the musicians on the record.

Now *Fathers and Sons* is a big seller. But to me this is the thing. That's a record. It said something about what was going on around me.

The most recent album out, *After the Rain,* features a very strange photo of Muddy on the cover clutching a frog and is another excursion into blues psychedelia that misuses Muddy's talents. He wants to get back to the roots for a change. He feels it is time that he did what he does best. Why imitate other styles when you have created one of your own that everyone else has copied?

I think I always will have my sound. It may not sound as good as it did with the real things—with new members and things—but it will be close enough to know that it's still me.
I'm thinking about cutting one with just two guitars and drums. I want to get a good blues sound. I'd like to have Jimmy Rodgers to back me up. We might get a good something going. If I had to have a harp blower I'd like for it to be someone like Walter Horton. I don't even want no bass on it. Let the guitar keep the bass. Cut a good old-timer. Too many pieces kindly interfere —two or three guitars, piano, harmonica—everyone fighting at one another. And I want to cut this blues at night. I like to cut my blues at night. It's the only time. Used to cut it at twelve o'clock at night. But everybody got so rich now they're at home asleep then. But at that time they was up with me.

Some of the younger Chicago bluesmen like Buddy Guy are doing their best to see that Muddy's music doesn't go down.

I would like to go in and do a good session behind Muddy. Me and Junior.

Buddy Guy and Junior Wells *(photo: David Gahr)*

And let Muddy do that stuff the way he's supposed to do. He can't feel this psychedelic stuff at all, and you've got to get that blues feeling into it. And if the feeling is gone, that's it. You can't get too busy behind a singer. You've got to let him sing it.

Muddy and Little Walter are the ones who started the band sound here in Chicago. And Muddy told me when I came here that if I wanted to go out on my own it would be hard. But he helped me and I worked on his records with him and that helped get me known. When I arrived in Chicago, Muddy, Walter, and Wolf were about the only blues bands going. Mostly in the clubs they were into a swinging, sort of a jazzy type thing, and I had to get onto that stuff to survive. But in time a lot of other blues groups like Junior and myself and Little Milton have come along, and we are carrying on their music. As long as I live I'll play Muddy's blues.

The black people are kept from this style of blues. They don't hear Muddy today on the radio or see him on television. And what you can't hear you'll never like. The white kids went out and got it, but the black people aren't exposed to the real blues. They have been taught that the blues is a low-class, gutbucket music and it wasn't good to go to this place or that place and they kept it like that for a long time. I came up with it all my life, and I'll always like it and play it. But I want to hear Muddy and John Lee Hooker and Lightning Hopkins on the radio too so we can all make a living like these English cats.

Although there is and probably always will be a blues scene in Chicago, it's not the way it used to be. Junior Wells, Buddy Guy, James Cotton, and Muddy are away more than they're home, playing the "white" jobs, touring in Europe or Africa, working the folk and blues festivals at Newport, Philadelphia, Ann Arbor, or Berkeley. The money is there today, not in the clubs, and the club scene just isn't what it was ten or fifteen years ago. The change has less to do with music than with the whole quality of life in the cities today. Muddy is acutely aware of what is going on.

When you get my age you've got to stay out of the clubs so regular. You go

in a club you're off twenty, you play forty. Kills you. Short pay. Long hours. Work six and half hours in a club, it's too long.
I used to think about running a club, but I'm too old for the club business. I couldn't be bothered with what all goes into a club. You have to have a good location, nice neighborhood. But like these gang-bangs going on here now, I couldn't be in a club, man. You got your thousands and thousands of dollars in the club, and they come in and run it like they want to run it. Run all your customers away. No, I couldn't even be bothered with that, man. It's too terrible now. There's too much going on. I don't know what's going to happen—gollee, man, I never seen nothing like this before. Getting too rough, man. It's always been a little rough. Ever since I remember, it was rough, but not like it is today. People beating on people, just to beat 'em. And killing 'em, shooting 'em. You're on your way home or probably on your way to the corner grocery store and somebody's gonna walk up and then, bam. That's too much. It's too much to go out any more. Just stay home and watch TV. Take it easy. It's too much. That Pepper's Lounge on Forty-third Street. I played there a long time and man, you didn't have standing room in there. But they tell me now they hardly ever have a decent crowd.
It's that way in every city. It's worse amongst my peoples—amongst the blacks. Whites got their gangs going too, you know, but they're not using it in the same way my people are—they're just going down the street shooting people. And that's what we used to do when we lived in the country—go rabbit hunting. You shoot rabbits. But you're shooting it for a cause. You're gonna eat that. But you go out in the street, BAM! Shit, man. Nobody wants to lose their life like that. What's going to happen next? You have to call the grocery store and they'll have to deliver your stuff. Then they'll get shot on the way. Then they'll close the store. But you've got to eat out of there. Too much dope going. Pills, LSD, Heroin—even got cough syrup they're taking here now. Them people's crazy—out of their minds.
And if there's no clubs where you can get your music together, it's rough. It's rough for young musicians who've got no scene going, you know. We had a good scene going here for music and now it's over. I don't know. If I was young and coming from Mississippi today I'd probably turn around and go back. And the audience loses too. It's better live instead of on records. There's just so many notes you got on that record. But when you're out there in person,

well you've got to put in different things that the record ain't even got.

Aware as he is that the level of despair and violence is rising around him, Muddy is also aware of pressures from the white world that contribute to that despair and violence.

Used to be out on the road, you had to find the black neighborhood and get a hotel somewhere in there, you know. 'Cause I know we went to a couple of hotels in small towns like Saginaw, Michigan, and everything and they said "We're filled up," you know, and you'd stand around a little bit and you'd see somebody come in and sign up. But that marching brought that down. You can get into most any hotel you want to. A few are still prejudiced, you know, but you can get in there, even if they don't like it. 'Cause number one, they're afraid to turn you down because they don't know who you is. You might be a Black Panther—ha, ha, ha—and burn it down to the ground—ha, ha, ha—I don't know, but I've never made sense with that stuff—I'm black but I never made sense with that kind of stuff—even from a kid on up. I don't know what the heck it was. What is this? Why should this be? What are people afraid of? I think it's their women they're afraid about. That's the whole point. That's the whole thing. Nothing wrong with messing with a black woman. That's fun to them. It's sick. I can't dig this. You're so particular about your woman, but my woman, you want to be able to do anything you want to do, and nobody say anything to you. And another thing in there is money. Jobs. They don't want to give anyone else a shot at it. Keep 'em out of there. That's the two basic things—women and money. It's more the lower-class people than the real rich people. 'Cause you know, none of 'em want you fooling with that woman. But like the poorer class people are the ones that are really stringed out.
I lived in the South. They need to patch up. They ain't patched up. They need to patch up. When you find this particular thing—when I first went North I wanted to know what the hell is all this about—when you could mix your women. Well, what's the difference? I ain't seen no difference. Man, it's just jelly between the biscuit or something. Gollee, killing people about

that crazy stuff, man. It's got 'em right now—someone shouting, "You're a nigger lover"—some of these sons of bitches are crazy. To each his own. If you love a nigger, you get you a nigger. If I love a white woman, I'll get me a white woman. I got to live with her, you ain't got to live with her. It's crazy, man, crazy.

It's better now, though, in the South. I was in Tennessee recently. Smooth sailing, man. Some came to the dance where I played at—to the club. White folks. Okay. Smooth sailing, but still I don't want to live there. I had my part of it. I got enough. I was there when it was rough. I don't give a damn how good it gets. I'll still stay here or some other big city. You got prejudice all over. Everywhere. Chicago, even New York. They got prejudiced people. But I don't pay it no attention. You're gonna find a rotten egg in every basket, so forget it. Live my own life.

But I got a feeling things ain't fixing to get right. I think they're gonna get worse. 'Cause there's more blacks going into this thing every day. Violence. And that's no good. That's no good. And all they do is put three policemen on the corner instead of one. And they don't spend no money to fix the city up. People would rather live in the city. They don't want to live out there. You can have the homes out there. Just fix it up. They're looking over our own cities. They go on down to Florida and try to build something up in the air. Hell, that's terrible. Little poor kids running round here now ain't hardly got food to eat. What I mean, let 'em open up the jobs. Ain't gonna give nobody nothing. Get it yourself. And these mothers who got kids without fathers, kindly straighten them out a little bit. They need a little help. 'Cause some people just want you to give 'em something. Hell. Away with that. James Brown says, "Open the door, I'll get it myself." We've been having trouble around here about these buildings—construction stuff, you know. Not enough blacks on there. They've been raising hell. What I mean it's so thin, anybody can see it—the white man gets all the good jobs. There's got to be something very bad got to be did before things turn around. I don't know what the hell it's gonna be.

Although he is troubled at what he sees going on around him, Muddy maintains much the same attitude toward life that he brought with him to Chicago.

157

BOSSMAN MUDDY WATERS

All he can do is what he does best: play the blues his way. In October of 1969 the car he was riding in was run into. Muddy's driver was killed and he was badly smashed up. Six months after the accident he is still on crutches and is trying to regain the lost feeling in his left hand—his fretting hand—which means it is difficult for him to play slide guitar. At fifty-five, many men would have given up, but the thought never entered his head. All he wants to do is get back out there and sing. It's his life. He's a professional.

I was blowing harmonica when I was fifteen. I'm fifty-five April 4. I've been on records twenty-some years. And I was playing years before I got on the records—or trying to play—whatever you might call it. Sounded good to me. Seems like to me I'm just about ten years in the business. I've never had a thought about giving it up. Before I was hurt I was strong and it seems like the older I get, the better I get. It's like I'm just starting to realize what it is. Unfortunate luck—that's nothing to worry about. I'm just thankful that I'm living. 'Cause there was a good shot there I could have went on out, you know.

to: David Gahr

AFTERWORD

Since I wrote this book in 1970, there have been many developments. Bill Monroe continues to play with vigor and creativity and maintains a schedule that would run many a younger man into the ground. In addition to the usual round of concerts and Bluegrass festivals, Bill has played at the White House, has appeared on most of the major television programs produced in Nashville, and has traveled extensively overseas in both Europe and Japan. He recently achieved his lifelong ambition of traveling to the Holy Land. Bill has also seen a whole new generation of artists like Ricky Skaggs, Emmylou Harris, Peter Rowan, and the Kentucky Headhunters take his music to a young audience. He had the pleasure of seeing his classic song "Uncle Pen" become a #1 record by Ricky Skaggs and was featured dancing in the video. He also became the first recipient of a Grammy for a Bluegrass recording.

Similarly, Muddy Waters lived to see his music achieve world-wide acceptance before his death in May of 1983. In addition to Paul Butterfield, Mike Bloomfield, Elvin Bishop, John Mayall, and The Rolling Stones, Johnny Winter and George Thorogood did much in recent years to reintroduce Muddy's music to a new audience of young listeners in this country and abroad. He died with the satisfaction of knowing that he had more than accomplished the goals he set for himself when he first came from Mississippi to Chicago. He had indeed become "a known person."

ABOUT THE AUTHOR

James Rooney has been involved in music ever since he first appeared on the WCOP "Hayloft Jamboree" as a teenager in Boston in 1954. He has been a musical partner of banjoist Bill Keith for thirty years. He was the manager of the Club 47 in Cambridge, Massachusetts in the mid-sixties and subsequently became a Director of the Newport Folk Festival. He then became the manager of the Bearsville Sound Studio in Woodstock, N.Y. In recent years he has been living in Nashville, Tennessee, where he is a member of Jack Clement's musical family. He divides his time between playing, engineering, and producing records. Together with Eric Von Schmidt he is the author of "Baby, Let Me Follow You Down: The Illustrated Story of the Cambridge Folk Years" (Doubleday/Anchor 1979).